HOW TO BE AN
Artist

Written by
S. Natalie Abadzis

Written by S. Natalie Abadzis
Consultants Leslie Primo, Jennifer Gibbs

Editor Sally Beets
Designers Charlotte Jennings,
Brandie Tully-Scott

Additional design Ann Cannings, Sonny Flynn,
Rachael Parfitt-Hunt, Sadie Thomas
Additional editorial Olivia Stanford
Illustrator Mark Ruffle
DTP designers Vijay Kandwal, Nityanand Kumar
Project picture researcher Rituraj Singh
Jacket co-ordinator Issy Walsh
Jacket designer Brandie Tully-Scott
Managing editor Jonathan Melmoth
Managing art editor Diane Peyton Jones
Production editor Abi Maxwell
Production controller Basia Ossowska
Creative director Helen Senior
Publishing director Sarah Larter

First published in Great Britain in China by
Dorling Kindersley Limited
80 Strand, London, WC2R 0RL

Copyright © 2021 Dorling Kindersley Limited
A Penguin Random House Company
10 9 8 7 6 5 4 3 2 1
001-322458-June/2021

A CIP catalogue record for this book
is available from the British Library.
ISBN: 978-0-2414-7411-2

Printed and bound in China

For the curious
www.dk.com

This book was made with Forest
Stewardship Council™ certified paper –
one small step in DK's commitment to
a sustainable future. For more information
go to www.dk.com/our-green-pledge

Contents

Hello there! It's wonderful to have you on board as we travel through the world of art. We will be discovering and trying out lots of different types of art, as well as meeting some amazing artists along the way.

My background as an artist and art teacher meant I was super excited to write this book. What better way to share my experience than with the artists and designers of the future? I've always found that I learn just as much from children as they learn from me. Young people have the best ideas!

Art links to other subjects too - there are lots of science and maths conundrums in art, and you will see that as you turn the pages of this book.

Art is for everybody. It inspires us to ask questions about ourselves and the world in which we live. What is it about art that excites you? What activities have you always wanted to try? This book encourages you to have a go and see what happens. You don't need lots of expensive materials to be an artist - a piece of paper and a pencil are great tools to start with.

One last thing to remember is that creating art is not about being perfect. It's about having ideas, experimenting, and trusting in the process. A bit of practice helps, too. Believe in yourself and the rest will follow.

I hope you have as much fun trying out the activities as I did when I wrote this book. Enjoy, make art, and feel inspired!

S. Nathreid Avady

How the book works

In *How to be an Artist,* you will learn how to think and act like an artist. The book is packed with fun activities that can be done at home, amazing art history, and a look at some of the most famous artists of all time.

Awesome activities

Get inspired and try out the fun activities in this book, which are based on key ideas within art. It's important to express yourself when being creative, so the finished crafts you create may not match those in the book exactly – but that's OK!

Everything you need for an activity is listed at the start.

Each activity is broken down into steps.

"Now try..." suggestions help you build on new knowledge.

Safety first

All of the projects in this book should be done with care. If you see this symbol at the top of a page, it means that you will need an adult to help you with the activity.

Take particular care when:

• you are using sharp objects, such as scissors

• you are using an oven

• you are outside – always tell an adult what you are doing

The introduction lets you know which area of art you're exploring.

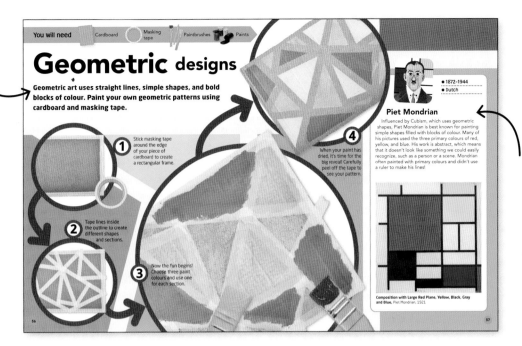

Feature boxes provide more information about the artist and art movement behind the activity.

Top topics

Learn about some of the most important art topics, such as colour, illustration, and pattern. These will support you as you explore your creative side when trying out the craft projects.

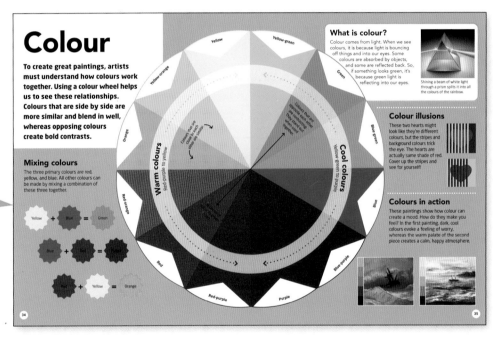

Amazing artists

The stories behind some of the greatest artists in history are brought to life in these pages. And remember: anyone can be an artist.

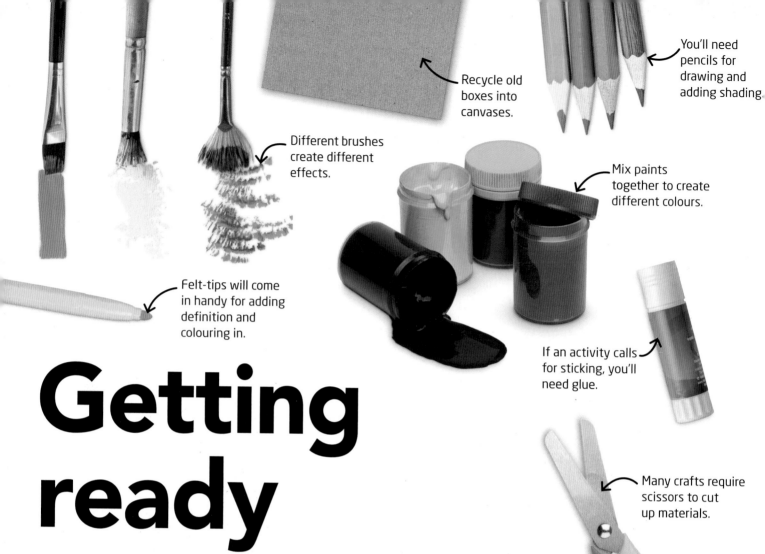

You'll need pencils for drawing and adding shading.

Recycle old boxes into canvases.

Mix paints together to create different colours.

Different brushes create different effects.

If an activity calls for sticking, you'll need glue.

Felt-tips will come in handy for adding definition and colouring in.

Many crafts require scissors to cut up materials.

Getting ready

You can dive straight into many of the projects in this book using equipment that you probably have at home. Here are some of the essential tools and techniques that will come in handy.

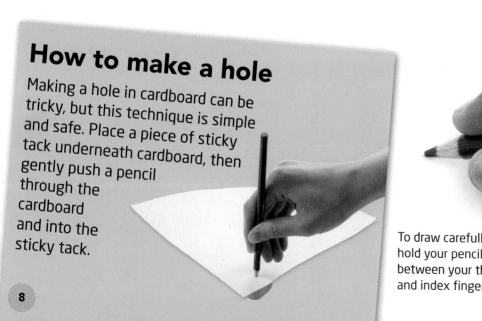

How to make a hole

Making a hole in cardboard can be tricky, but this technique is simple and safe. Place a piece of sticky tack underneath cardboard, then gently push a pencil through the cardboard and into the sticky tack.

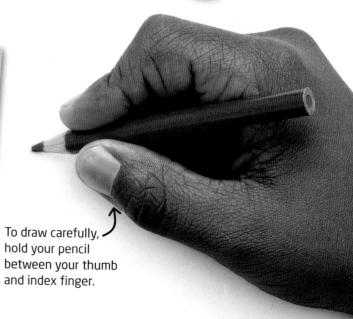

To draw carefully, hold your pencil between your thumb and index finger.

Thinking like an artist

Some people think they can't be an artist because they find drawing or painting tricky, but anybody can be creative! The key is to have a positive "can do" attitude. Here are some tips to get into an artistic mindset:

1 Get curious. Art is all about asking questions. What do you want to communicate with your artwork?

2 Whether it's the outdoors, a trip to a gallery, or a film, find out what inspires you and immerse yourself in it.

3 Let your imagination run free. Art made without a plan can go in interesting and surprising directions.

4 Notice art in the world around you. What patterns, beauty, or shapes can you spot on your journey to school?

5 Don't be afraid to play, experiment, and make mistakes. The process is as important as the final result.

6 Practise, practise, practise! Hardly anyone is happy with their first try. It takes time to improve your skills.

Tracing

You can transfer a shape or net from pages 134-135 onto paper or card by tracing it. You'll need tracing paper, a sharp pencil, a soft graphite pencil (such as 6B) and the steps below.

1 Place the tracing paper over the shape and draw over the lines using any pencil.

2 Flip the tracing paper. Shade over the back of the lines with a soft graphite pencil.

3 Place the tracing paper, shaded side down, onto the paper or card you're tracing onto.

4 Pressing down with a sharp pencil, draw over the lines of the shape to transfer it.

Composition

Sketching

3D drawing

Illustration

Drawing

You don't need expensive equipment or materials to make a drawing. It begins with an idea, then a mark on paper. Whether it's doing a simple doodle or sketching a portrait, everyone can learn to draw.

Self-portraits

Tone

Ideas

Perspective

Ideas

Every piece of art begins with a spark of inspiration, but where do these ideas come from? Many artists experience the "fear of the blank page", and so they use different techniques to get started. Read this to learn about some of the ways to feel inspired!

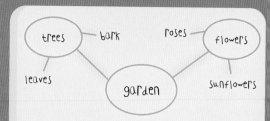

Mind mapping

Create a mind map by writing your main idea in the middle circle. Expand this bit by bit, until you have many options to choose from.

Experiences

Making art from your memories and experiences is a good place to start. It can help you to respond to how a specific memory made you feel, process difficult experiences, or even just record a special event.

Seeking inspiration

There are many things you can do to help find inspiration - from going on a walk or doing some gardening, to visiting an art gallery or museum.

Eureka!

Sometimes ideas just come to you, as if from nowhere! Train your brain to be open to these moments by keeping curious. Question the world around you by using the "five Ws" – who, what, where, why, and when – and see what happens!

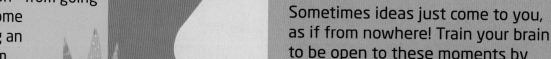

The power of practising

There's truth in "practice makes perfect". In 1888, Vincent van Gogh practised painting **The Sunflowers** many times before he was happy with the effect. Careful observation and practice will help to get your ideas right.

 Now try...

Making a mini sketchbook

This little book will be the perfect place to keep track of your ideas, thoughts, and notes.

You will need

 Paper and card   Safety scissors   Elastic band

1. Make a cover from card and decorate it however you like. Fold it in half.

2. Fold sheets of A4 paper in half and slot them inside the cover.

3. Lace an elastic band over the cover, to hold the pages inside the book.

You could paint or draw a design onto the front of your notebook.

The news

Many artists put their ideas out into society in response to the events going on at the time. Some hope to inspire change, or to draw attention to certain issues.

Composition game

Composition is the way different shapes and objects are placed to fit together in an artwork. Create a composition with this fun game!

1 Draw a 7x7 grid like the one below.

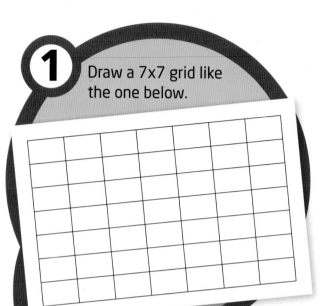

2 Fill in your grid with different types of things that can make up an image. Choose any categories you like, and draw different examples. See below for inspiration.

	1	2	3	4	5	6
Sky	clouds	sun	rain clouds	moon and stars	birds	rainbow
Background	hills	mountains	horizon	horizon	sea	city skyline
Foreground	monkey	path	whale	desert	monster	road
Plants	palm trees	tree	cactus	bushes	leaves	pine trees
Buildings	skyscrapers	hut	igloo	tent	apartments	house
Transport	car	camel	fishing boat	hot-air balloon	bus	bicycle

The foreground is the part of the picture that seems nearest to you. Draw things in the foreground larger and in the lower half of the picture.

4

Your finished drawing should look something like this!

Choose a category, roll the dice, then draw the image that matches that number in the column. Remember to leave space for other parts of the picture as you go along.

3

→ # Now try...

Building a bizarre body

Have a go at creating some peculiar art with friends by folding a piece of paper into four, then passing it between you, taking turns to draw each part of a figure. This activity is based on a game created by a group of artists in the 1920s, called the "Exquisite Corpse", in which each artist drew a different section of a body without seeing the others. The end results could be very strange!

Elements
of art

There are many different artistic elements that work together to create an effect. Lines, shapes, colours, patterns, and more all give a picture different qualities. You can use a mix of elements to create your own individual style.

Patterns are repeating designs, such as spots or stripes. Turn to page 52 to find out more.

Pattern

Colours make a picture bright and eye-catching. Discover more on page 34.

Colour

Line

A line is a mark longer than a dot. It can be thick or thin, straight or curved, wiggly or angular, long or short. Lines can also be joined up to make shapes.

Line

Texture

Texture is how a surface feels to touch, and it can be hard to capture in a drawing. A good way to practise is by trying to copy very different textures, such as a shiny spoon or a woolly jumper.

Texture

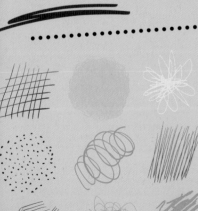

Shape

A shape is created by an outline and looks flat. Shapes may be filled with a colour to make them stand out. Geometric shapes are well defined, such as squares or triangles.

Form

A form is a three-dimensional (3D) shape. You can create different forms by adding shading to shapes.

Shape

Form

Sunlight

Shading helps a flat shape look 3D.

Space

Tone

Space

Space is the area inside or around a shape. How you place shapes and how big they are will change how your picture feels. The space between shapes can be as important as the shapes themselves.

Tone

Tone is how light or dark a picture is. Changing the tone within a shape by adding shading can make that shape look 3D. You can create a whole painting using different tones of just one colour.

The Swiss-German artist Paul Klee once said that "a drawing is simply a line going for a walk". Try this out yourself by doodling freely with a pen and seeing what shapes appear.

Take a line...
...for a walk

1 Take your pen for a walk! Fill the paper with simple swirls, loops, and lines to split it up into sections.

2 Use felt-tips to fill in the shapes you've created with different patterns and blocks of colour.

3 Create more doodles on different pieces of paper and place them next to each other to create a tiled effect.

Doodling for calm

Have you ever sat down with a colouring book or made marks on paper without planning it? Drawing is a simple way to relax – try it next time you feel stressed. Aim to concentrate on nothing but the pen on the page. It might make you feel more mindful, which means focusing on the moment.

How to draw a face

Many artists have created portraits throughout history. Even though we look at faces every day, it's trickier than it seems to draw them! Follow these steps to discover a quick and easy way to draw a face.

Use a ruler to draw a faint line down the middle of the oval, then sketch a horizontal line halfway down.

 1 Look in the mirror and lightly sketch an oval outline of your face onto a piece of paper.

2

Add another horizontal line halfway between the middle line and the bottom of the page, and then another slightly below it.

3 Draw the eyes, nose, and mouth using the lines to guide you. The top of the ears should sit at the same level as the eyes.

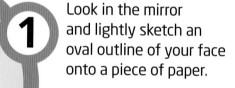
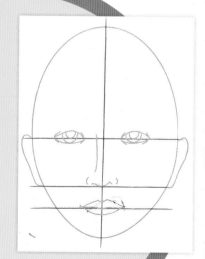

Now try...

Have a go at quick portraits of your pets. Follow the steps on the right to sketch a simple cat picture.

Drawing a cat portrait

1 Start with the tail

2 Then add ears and whiskers.

3 Finally, add the legs and face.

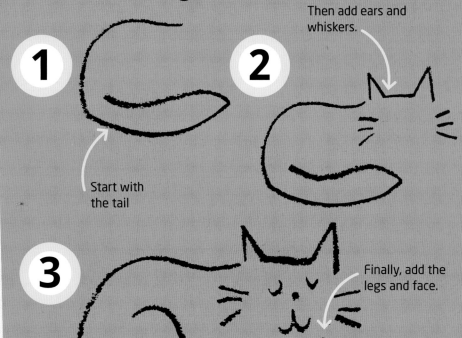

4 Rub out the lines. Draw on some hair and a neck, then colour in your portrait.

Mona Lisa

This portrait is on display at the Louvre, Paris. It became famous when, in 1911, it was stolen! While it was missing, people visited the museum to view the empty space on the wall. It was eventually found in 1913. It's the most valuable painting in the world.

Mona Lisa, Leonardo da Vinci 1503-1516

Albrecht Dürer

Artist • 1471–1528 • German

Albrecht Dürer honed his artistic talents by practising observational drawing. He became a master mathematician, engraver, and painter, and even built his own "drawing machines" that he used to make his art more realistic.

Albrecht Dürer's 1484 self-portrait

Self-portrait pro

Albrecht Dürer initially worked with his father as a goldsmith (a metal worker), but he begged his father to let him train as an artist. Finally, his dad gave in. Dürer drew his first self-portrait when he was just 13 years old. He went on to become one of the most talented portrait painters of his time.

Rhinoceros, Albrecht Dürer, 1515

Wonderful woodcuts

Dürer is best-known for his woodcuts. Woodcutting is the oldest form of printing, created by cutting a picture into wood, then printing it onto paper. One of Dürer's most famous woodcuts is the rhinoceros seen here on the left – but he'd never actually seen the animal! He created it from what he'd read about them and by using his imagination. Do you think it looks like a real rhino?

Master of perspective and proportion

Perspective is a technique Dürer used to make pictures look more realistic and like they had depth. He also made his art accurate by studying the body. He realized that certain parts were the same size in relation, or proportion, to others, such as the width of the hand and face.

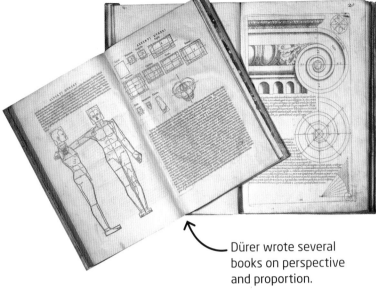

Dürer wrote several books on perspective and proportion.

"Without proportion, no picture can ever be perfect."

Drawing machine

In the 15th century, artists such as Dürer built perspective machines that helped them to draw scenes more accurately. By looking through a grid, they could concentrate on each section of a scene so that each was drawn in proportion to the rest of the picture.

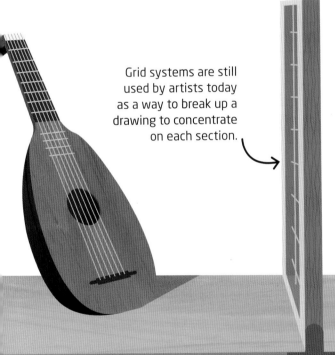

Grid systems are still used by artists today as a way to break up a drawing to concentrate on each section.

Tricking
the eye

Optical illusions play tricks with your mind by confusing the way you see patterns and shapes. An image might appear to move, to connect together in impossible ways, or look 3D. Try this simple hole illusion.

Draw a circle. Then draw smaller circles inside it, the line of each one beginning in the same place.

Use a black pen to colour in alternate rings, as shown.

Op Art movement

Around the 1960s, some artists created optical illusions that tricked our eyes. This is called Op Art. "Op" is short for "optical".

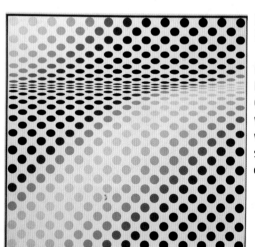

Hesitate,
Bridget Riley, 1964

British artist Bridget Riley's first Op Art paintings were black and white and used simple shapes like circles and lines.

3 Add shading with a pencil to the left side of the circles. This will add tone, which will then create the optical illusion of the hole getting deeper.

Try it out!

Test your brain with these optical illusions. At first glance, the image on the left may look like a real triangle, but look again. Its sides appear to be in front and behind one another at the same time! On the right is a moving-image illusion – as you look at the picture, it appears to be moving.

Penrose triangle

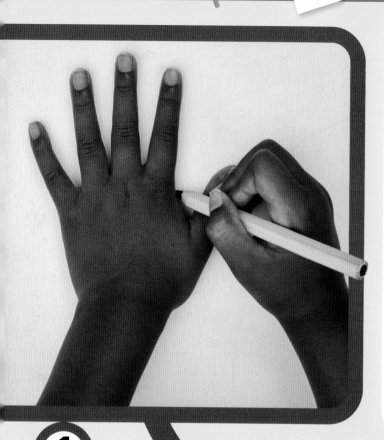

Handy
3D drawing

Impress your friends by trying out this neat trick. With this simple technique, you can make a flat drawing of your hand look like a solid 3D object!

1

Lay your non-writing hand flat on a piece of paper and draw around it with a pencil.

With a felt-tip, draw a straight line across the sheet of paper, curving it when you reach the inside of the hand outline. When you reach the other side of the outline, go back to drawing a straight line. Repeat, using a different colour for each line.

2

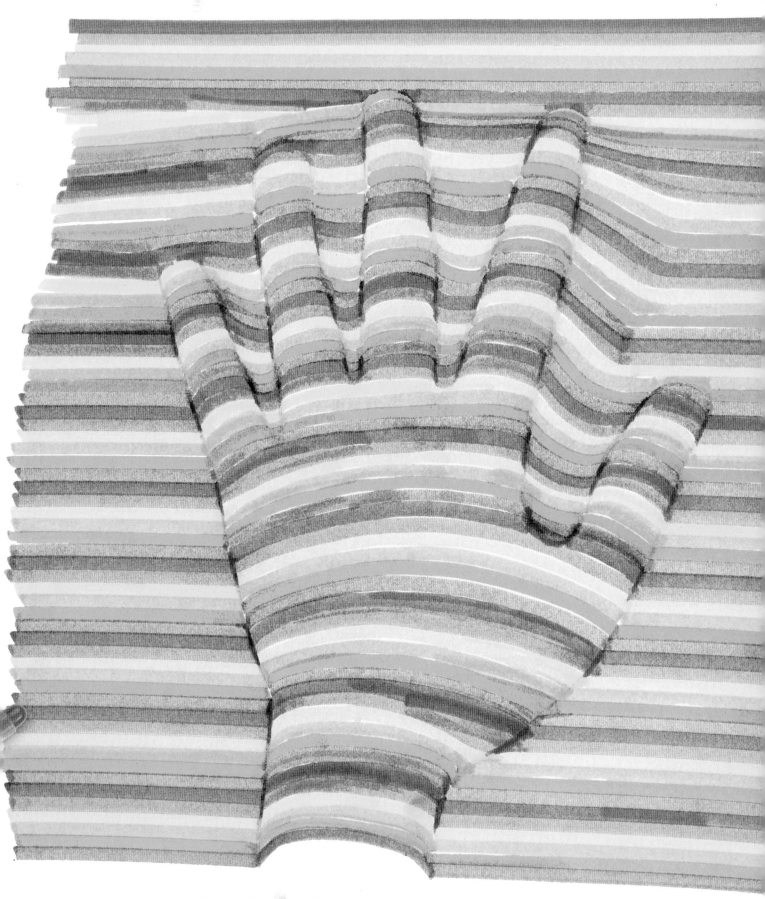

Continue drawing
the coloured lines until
you've completed
the whole hand!

1 Draw a straight line horizontally across a blank piece of paper – this is the "horizon line". Next add a dot on this line – this is the "vanishing point".

2 Use a ruler to draw several lines from the vanishing point to the edges of the paper. These lines will help you place your objects.

Perspective

Drawing with perspective gives a sense of depth and makes the viewer feel as if they are in the picture! By making objects at the bottom bigger and objects in the top smaller, the artist can trick the viewer's eye into seeing a realistic view.

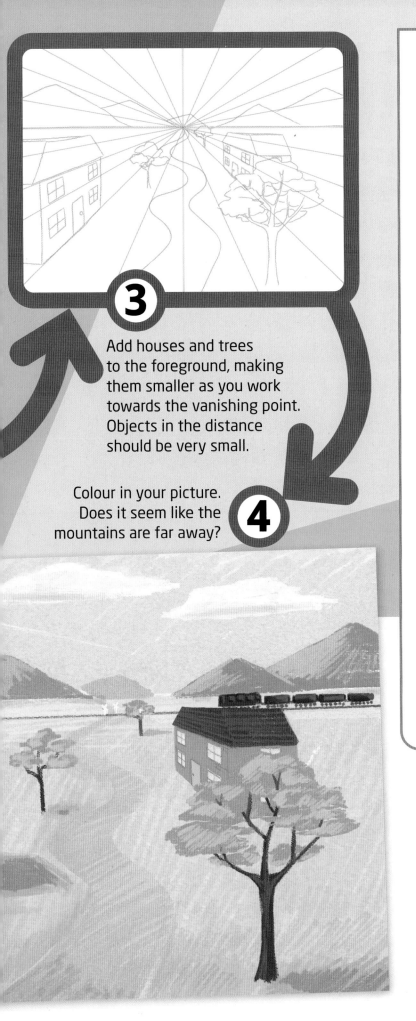

③

Add houses and trees to the foreground, making them smaller as you work towards the vanishing point. Objects in the distance should be very small.

Colour in your picture. Does it seem like the mountains are far away?

④

Vanishing point

If you have a clear view into the distance, you will notice buildings and other objects appear to get smaller as they get further away, and lead to a "vanishing point" where you can't see them any more.

Pairs of points

A picture can have more than one vanishing point. Can you spot where the vanishing points are in the image below? This is known as "two-point perspective".

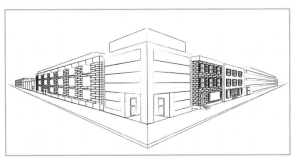

Now try...

Take a photo of a view and try drawing it. Can you find the vanishing point in the photo you've taken?

Illustration

An illustration is an artwork that's designed to go with words in books, posters, websites, and more. Illustrations can be drawn using different methods, such as with pencil on paper or designing on a computer.

Illustrators may work at home or in a professional studio.

Book illustrations

Many people enjoy stories more when there are illustrations to go with them. Usually the pictures are drawn by an illustrator, but sometimes the author of the story draws them too. Here are two examples.

Alice in Wonderland by Lewis Carroll, illustrated by Arthur Rackham, 1907

Songs of Innocence and Experience, "Infant Joy", William Blake, 1789

Mark Ruffle

Mark Ruffle is a digital illustrator, which means he creates illustrations using computer software. Mark studied Graphic Design at university, then got a job designing books. He now enjoys working as an illustrator, drawing cool stuff for children's books – including this one!

- Born in 1973
- British

What does an illustrator do?

An illustrator's job is to create pictures and images that make text easier to understand or help tell a story. Many illustrators specialize in a certain style, such as cartoons for children's books or scientific drawings for text books. Some illustrators create comics or graphic novels.

Pages from *Hortus Eystettensis* Basilius Besler, 1616

Scientific illustrations

Detailed drawings of complicated plants and animals are very useful for people studying science. Botanical illustrations can show the different parts of plants very clearly.

Advertisements

Illustrations can be used to help sell things. Illustrators create images for movie posters, adverts for products in magazines, and tempting pictures for food packaging.

Example of a poster advertising food

Digital illustrations

Nowadays, many artists can draw illustrations using software on computers, tablets, and even phones.

Characters from a Japanese comic book, also known as Manga

Comics and graphic novels

Comic books and graphic novels rely on strips of illustrations, sometimes with speech bubbles, to tell their stories. Comic books tell stories in short instalments, while graphic novels are longer and in book form.

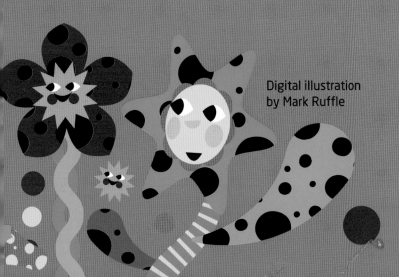

Digital illustration by Mark Ruffle

Graffiti

Pattern

Geometric shapes

Pointillism

Printing

Canvas

Colour mixing

Abstract art

Painting

From the cave paintings of ancient times through to modern art movements, people have always painted to express themselves. Whatever you choose to paint, it can be done on just about any surface, such as paper, canvas, or even, with permission, the walls of a building.

Colour

To create great paintings, artists must understand how colours work together. Using a colour wheel helps us to see these relationships. Colours that are side by side are more similar and blend in well, whereas opposing colours create bold contrasts.

Mixing colours

The three primary colours are red, yellow, and blue. All other colours can be made by mixing a combination of these three together.

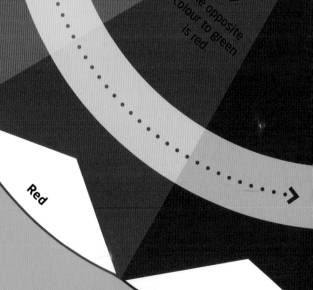

Yellow + Blue = Green

Blue + Red = Purple

Red + Yellow = Orange

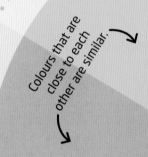

Yellow

Yellow-orange

Orange

Warm colours
Red-purple to yellow

Red-orange

Red

Red-purple

Colours that are close to each other are similar.

The opposite colour to green is red.

What is colour?

Colour comes from light. When we see colours, it is because light is bouncing off things and into our eyes. Some colours are absorbed by objects, and some are reflected back. So, if something looks green, it's because green light is reflecting into our eyes.

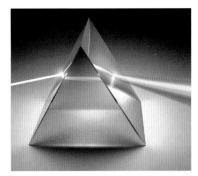

Shining a beam of white light through a prism splits it into all the colours of the rainbow.

Colour illusions

These two hearts might look like they're different colours, but the stripes and background colours trick the eye. The hearts are actually the same shade of red. Cover up the stripes and see for yourself!

Colours in action

These paintings show how colour can create a mood. How do they make you feel? In the first painting, dark, cool colours evoke a feeling of worry, whereas the warm palate of the second piece creates a calm, happy atmosphere.

Yellow-green

Green

Blue-green

Blue

Blue-purple

Purple

Cool colours
Yellow-green to purple

Colours that are opposite each other are contrasting. They stand out when used together.

Colour mixing arrays

The best way to learn about colour mixing is to try it out yourself! Discover what happens when you mix primary colours together, and afterwards use the amazing array of colours to reveal a secret picture.

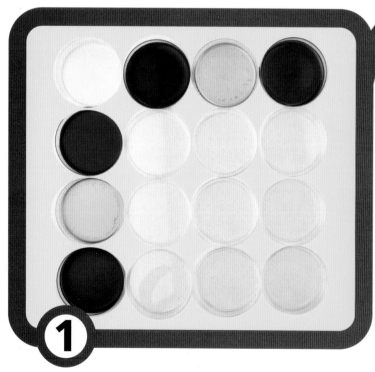

①

Set up your glasses like this (or use an ice cube tray). Drop the red, yellow, and blue food colouring into separate glasses around the outside.

2 Place your finger on the end of a straw and dip it into a primary colour. Drop a few droplets into each row or column that the colour is in. Use a different straw for each colour.

3 Pour a little bit of water into each of the new mixtures. Now you've got a set of brand new paints to use!

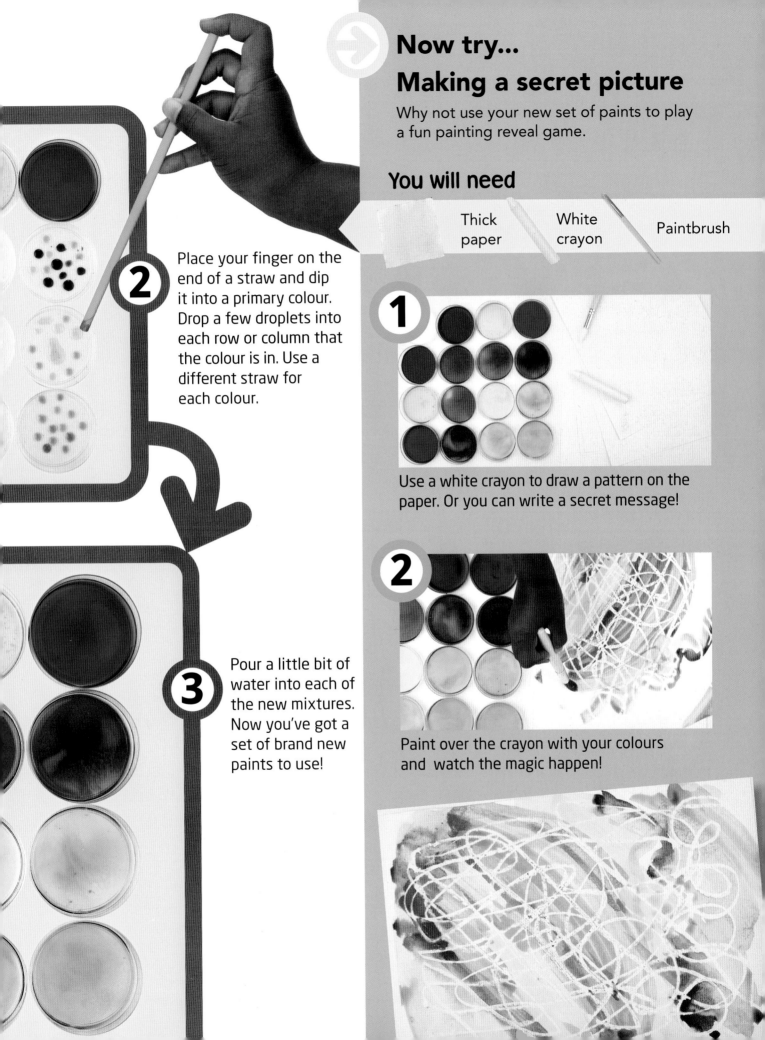

Now try...
Making a secret picture

Why not use your new set of paints to play a fun painting reveal game.

You will need

Thick paper	White crayon	Paintbrush

1 Use a white crayon to draw a pattern on the paper. Or you can write a secret message!

2 Paint over the crayon with your colours and watch the magic happen!

Walking rainbow

In this exciting experiment you can watch coloured water "walk". It also shows how the primary colours of red, yellow, and blue mix to create secondary colours.

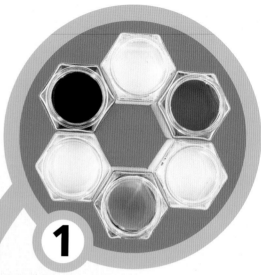

1

Fill six jars with water, then add a few drops of red, yellow, and blue food colouring into three of them. Alternate the jars holding clear water with the jars of coloured water – like this.

Real rainbows

A rainbow appears when sunlight shines through falling rain. Rain and sunlight together cause light to bend and split into the different colours. The colours you can usually see in a rainbow are red, orange, yellow, green, blue, indigo, and violet.

Tear six strips of kitchen roll and fold each one into a narrow strip.

Can you see all seven colours in this rainbow?

2

Place the end of a kitchen roll strip into one jar, and the other end into the jar next to it, ensuring both ends are touching the water. Repeat with the next jar.

Now try...

Food-colouring flowers

Fill a drinking glass a quarter of the way up with water and then add a few drops of food colouring. Cut the end off the stem of the flower and put it in the water. You will see the petals gradually turn the colour that you mixed into the water.

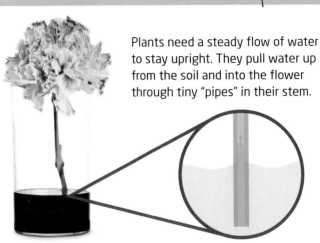

Plants need a steady flow of water to stay upright. They pull water up from the soil and into the flower through tiny "pipes" in their stem.

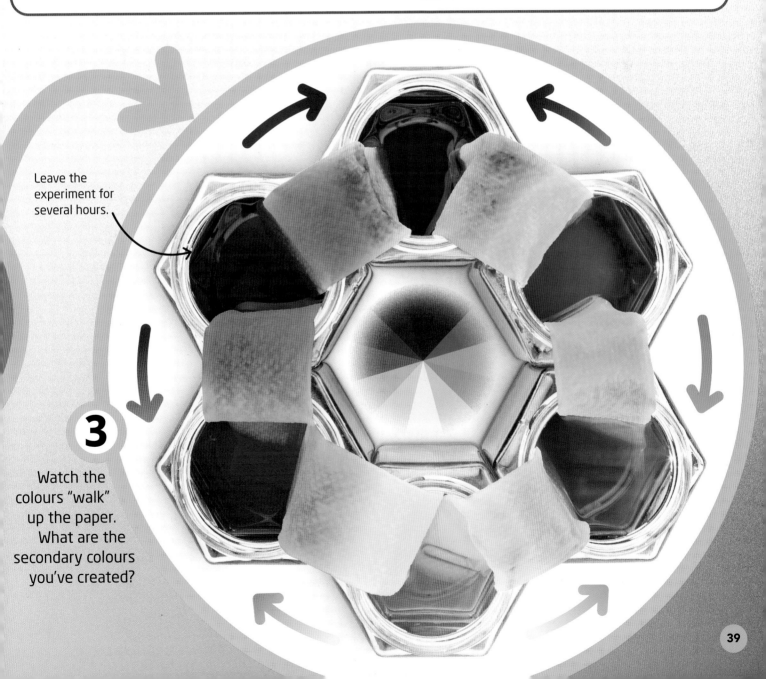

Leave the experiment for several hours.

3

Watch the colours "walk" up the paper. What are the secondary colours you've created?

Street art

Street art can be spotted in cities and towns around the world. Producing it in a public place means that it gets seen by many people, but there are some who disapprove because the artists don't always ask for permission, while others simply find it messy.

Making a mark

Many street artists leave their personal symbol, known as a tag, as graffiti. Have a go at designing your own – it could be your name, initials, a word, or a symbol. But do it on a piece of paper rather than a wall, unless you have special permission.

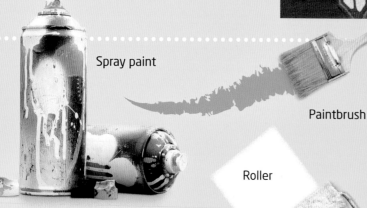

Spray paint

Paintbrush

Roller

Tools

Street artists use many tools to achieve different effects. Some paint "free hand", while others use stencils to create a neater result.

Earliest art on Earth

The *Cueva de las Manos* (or Cave of Hands) is one of the earliest examples of wall art and is located in Santa Cruz, Argentina. The hands were created thousands of years ago. Ancient people carved animal bones into pipes, which they used to blow paint over their hands, creating a stencilled effect on the cave wall.

The Berlin Wall

The Wolves, Jean-Michel Basquiat, 1982

Street politics

Many graffiti artists use their work to send a powerful political message, often by combining words and images. Jean-Michel Basquiat was a Black American artist, poet, and musician from New York City who began his career as a graffiti artist. He used symbols and words to create art about racism, poverty, and identity. "I don't think about art while I work," he once said. "I think about life."

The Berlin Wall

For 30 years, the city of Berlin was split between two countries and divided by a wall. Eventually, in 1989, the wall was torn down and the two countries united to become Germany. What was left of it is now covered in graffiti, making it the largest outdoor gallery in the world.

Banksy

Banksy is a famous British graffiti artist – but his identity is a secret! His work is thought-provoking and often humorous, based on events that are going on in the world. He uses stencils to quickly create artworks overnight.

● **Born in 1974**

● **British**

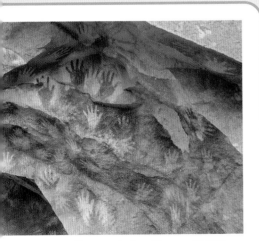

Cueva de las Manos, 7,300 BCE

The Flower Thrower, Banksy, 2003

Evolving canvas

This activity is all about taking your time. Create layers on a canvas using different tools such as sponges, rollers, brushes – anything you can paint with! Slowly, you'll build up an interesting picture.

1

Place a canvas, or big sheet of paper, outside – or anywhere it's OK to get messy!

Try sticking string or other objects onto your picture.

Try smudging the paint with a sponge – what effect does this create?

Choose colours that complement each other.

2

Spill, dab, and brush paint on to your canvas. Have fun with it!

Different tools will create different textures.

42

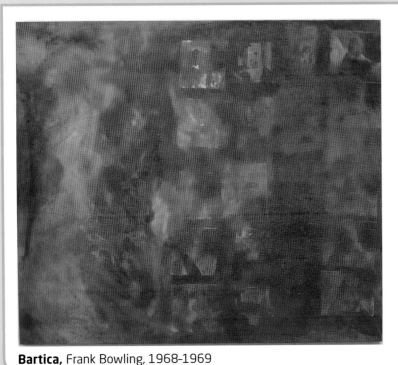

Bartica, Frank Bowling, 1968–1969

● Born in 1934
● British-Guyanese

Sir Frank Bowling

Frank was born in Guyana in South America. His style is abstract, so his art does not look like things from real life. He is known for his large pictures, for pouring paint onto the canvas, and for sticking small objects, such as toys, onto his works, that he sometimes paints over. His paintings are often very bold and colourful.

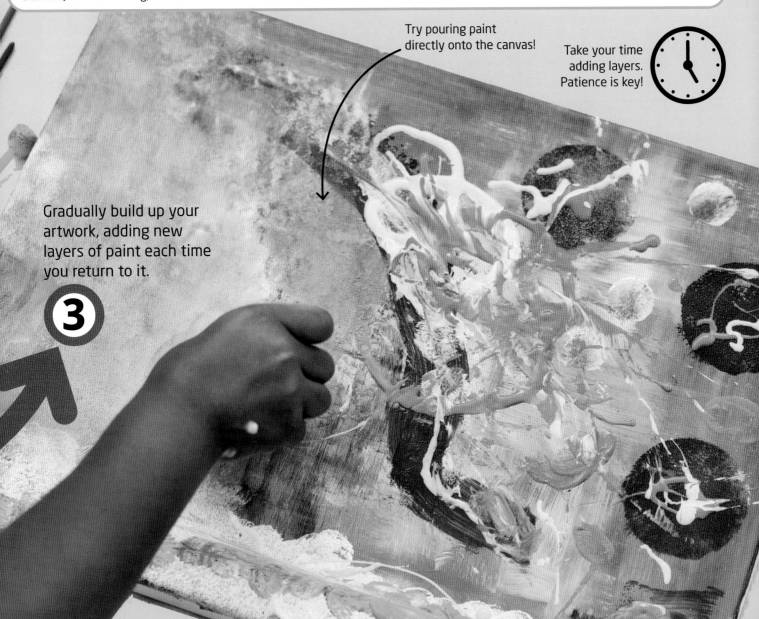

Try pouring paint directly onto the canvas!

Take your time adding layers. Patience is key!

Gradually build up your artwork, adding new layers of paint each time you return to it.

③

1 Use a pencil and ruler to split the canvas or paper into four sections, then choose four different pieces of music to paint to.

Use a ruler

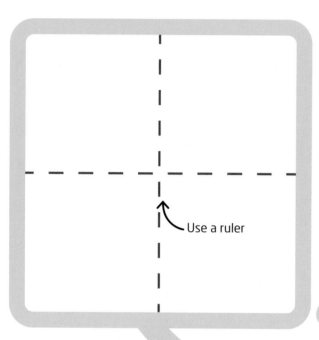

2

Play one piece of music at a time and paint inside one quarter for each sound. Try to paint in a way that feels natural to the sound.

Painting to
music

Do you like listening to music? Music can influence your mood and even inspire you. Try out this experiment to see how different music affects you artistically.

When you've finished, look at the different boxes. How do they compare with each other? Have you used different colours or brush strokes? How does each square make you feel?

3

Music and art

Many artists use sound and music in their work. In 1952, the artist John Cage recorded 4:33 minutes of silence just to make his audience think about what people could hear during that time. Wassily Kandinsky was a Russian abstract artist who had something called "synaesthesia", which means he could see sound and hear colour.

Composition 7, Wassily Kandinsky, 1913

Frida **Kahlo**

Painter • 1907–1954 • Mexican

Despite being in pain for most of her life, Frida Kahlo managed to produce some groundbreaking art. She's famous for her striking self-portraits, her flamboyant fashion sense, for fighting for her beliefs, and for expressing suffering through art.

Painting through pain

Frida's life was marked by pain and illness. She had a disease called polio when she was six, which meant she spent a lot of time alone, losing herself in drawing. Then, when she was a teenager, Frida was left with serious injuries following a bus crash. It was while recovering from her accident that she once again immersed herself in art - this time teaching herself to paint. Frida's suffering is visible in many of her paintings, which show her in surreal, sometimes frightening scenes.

During Frida's initial recovery period, her mum had a special easel made so Frida could paint in bed.

Portrait pro

Of Frida's 143 paintings, 55 are self-portraits. These paintings usually show Frida with a blank expression on her face, wearing bright clothes, and with dark hair piled on top of her head.

What do you think Frida is trying to tell us by including an image of a skull on her forehead?

The thorns in the background here could refer to pain, but the green leaves suggest growth.

"I am not sick. I am broken. But I am happy to be alive as long as I can paint."

Fashion icon

Frida expressed her Mexican heritage proudly by wearing brightly coloured embroidered clothes and placing flowers in her hair, in the style of the indigenous Tehuana women of Mexico.

Frida's colourful clothes, on display at a museum

Art and emotion

Sometimes people find it tricky to put their feelings into words. Creating art can help to process difficult events, memories, and emotions. Drawing or painting can help people to feel calmer and also create an escape if they are experiencing a low mood.

Lots of dots

Throughout history, artists have used little dots to make patterns. Have a go yourself by creating a dot art animal. Dab paint dots onto a rock for the body, then fix it to an outline to complete the animal.

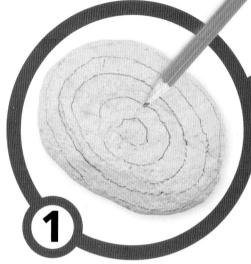

1

Choose whether you want your animal to be a turtle or a snail. Then, use a pencil to outline a simple pattern onto a rock.

Georges Seurat

French artist Georges Seurat came up with a method of painting called "pointillism". He used lots of tiny dots of different colours, which when looked at from a distance seem to blend together to make new colours. This is known as "optical mixing".

- 1859–1891
- French

A Sunday Afternoon on the Island of La Grande Jatte,
Georges Seurat, 1884–1886

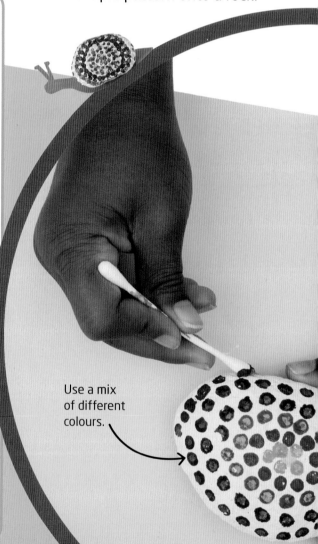

Use a mix of different colours.

Australian art

Australian First Nations people lived in Australia long before anyone else, and they still live there today. Their way of life has continued for thousands of years. Australian First Nations artists create artwork that represents their environment. They often use dotted paint to create symbols and patterns that tell stories.

An Australian First Nations artist painting

The rock will be the animal's shell.

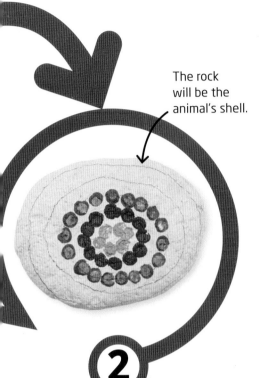

2

Dip the cotton bud or pencil end into paint and carefully dab dots along the lines.

3 Turn to page 135 to trace and cut out the animal outline. Place your rock on top of it.

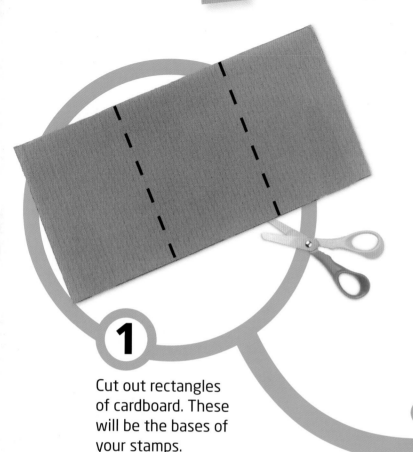

1

Cut out rectangles of cardboard. These will be the bases of your stamps.

Stick recycled objects with different textures and shapes onto the stamps. Let the glue dry. Then paint the objects on your stamps.

2

You can also use objects without bases, such as bubble wrap or a cork.

Wrapping paper printing

You can recycle and reuse items you no longer need to create unique wrapping paper. Mix up the shapes and colours to make a personal print perfect for wrapping presents!

3

Take a piece of paper big enough to wrap your gift, then press your painted stamps onto it. You can also dip an object, such as a cork, in paint to make an individual stamp.

Any type of paper will do, but sugar paper works well.

4

Let the paint dry and you're ready to wrap your present! You could even make a printed card to go with it.

Try using one colour for each different shape to make a pattern.

Pattern

A pattern is a design of repeated lines, shapes, or colours arranged in a particular way. Different patterns can be put together to create an artwork. You can spot patterns everywhere, both in nature and in art.

Symmetrical patterns

Symmetry is when a shape or pattern is repeated inside itself. There are two types: reflective and rotational. Reflective symmetry means that when you fold a pattern in half, both sides are the same. Rotational symmetry means that when you spin a pattern around its centre, it looks the same.

This rangoli pattern, made using sand as part of Hindu celebrations, shows rotational symmetry. The same pattern repeats six times.

Tessellating patterns

Tessellation is an artistic technique in which repeating shapes are fitted together like a jigsaw. Creating a tessellating pattern uses maths skills, as it involves working out how a shape will fill a space.

A pattern is made when objects or shapes are organized in a repeated sequence.

Why our brains see patterns

Spotting patterns helps us to connect our thoughts together and make sense of the world. Can you see a face in the tree bark to the right? Next time you are outside, see what patterns you can spot!

The pattern on this vase has reflective symmetry. If you drew a line down the middle, the pattern would be mirrored on the left and right.

Yinka Shonibare

Yinka Shonibare's artwork explores culture, history, and human migration (people moving to other countries). In 2014, he covered 6,000 books in wax print fabric, which is popular for clothing in parts of Africa but often made abroad, to make people think about the history of the material. Many of the books were written by authors whose families had moved to Britain.

- Born in 1962
- British-Nigerian

The British Library, Yinka Shonibare, 2014

Geometric tiles are used to make beautiful mosaics in Islamic art.

Geometric patterns

Geometric patterns are made up of repeating geometric shapes such as squares, rectangles, and triangles. Islamic art traditionally uses geometric patterns. Colourful tiles are often used to decorate mosques with intricate designs.

Ndebele patterns

Artist Esther Mahlangu is from the Ndebele nation in South Africa, where it's tradition to decorate the outside of your home. You can paint your own Ndebele house in Mahlangu's bold style.

Dr. Esther Mahlangu

Esther Mahlangu was taught to paint by her mother and grandmother. Her patterns take inspiration from the clothing and jewellery of the Ndebele people, and are very colourful and geometric.

- Born in 1935
- South African

Ndebele Abstract, Esther Mahlangu, 2019

1

Use a ruler to draw lines along the card, creating rectangular sections. Then draw some diagonal and horizontal lines to make smaller shapes, leaving out the rectangle in the middle and on the right-hand side.

Fill in the shapes with bright paints. Use brown for the middle rectangle to make it look like a door. Leave to dry.

2

54

Dazzling designs

When Mahlangu first began painting, she used natural materials such as clay and charcoal. Paints are easier to buy now, so her paintings have become more and more bright and colourful!

Ndebele house

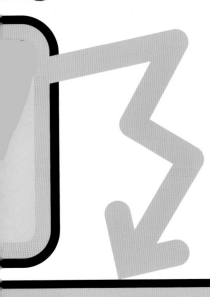

Go over your patterns with a black pen and add more stripes and lines.

3

Esther Mahlangu has used a chicken feather to paint!

To make a roof, create a cone shape by following the instructions on page 64. Then snip around the edges of it to make a fringe. Create another cone for a double-layered effect!

 Leave this section bare, as you will glue here.

4

Curve the card into a cylinder and glue it together.

Create an open door by cutting up and across the door outline.

Geometric designs

Geometric art uses straight lines, simple shapes, and bold blocks of colour. Paint your own geometric patterns using cardboard and masking tape.

1 Stick masking tape around the edge of your piece of cardboard to create a rectangular frame.

2 Tape lines inside the outline to create different shapes and sections.

3 Now the fun begins! Choose three paint colours and use one for each section.

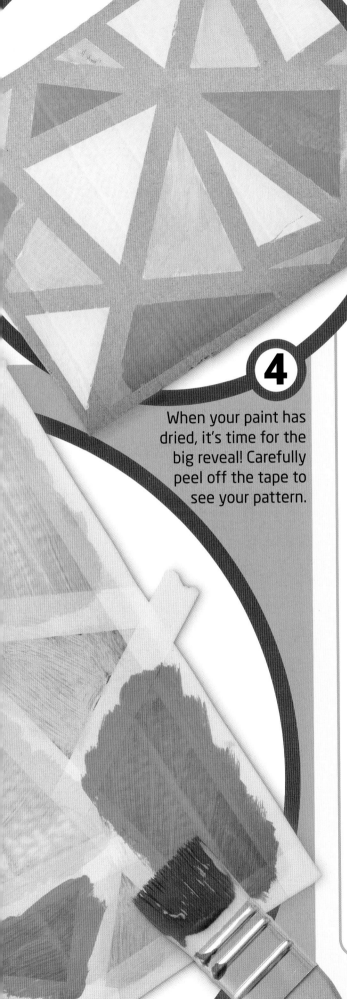

4

When your paint has dried, it's time for the big reveal! Carefully peel off the tape to see your pattern.

● 1872-1944
● Dutch

Piet Mondrian

Influenced by Cubism, which uses geometric shapes, Piet Mondrian is best known for painting simple shapes filled with blocks of colour. Many of his pictures used the three primary colours of red, yellow, and blue. His work is abstract, which means that it doesn't look like something we could easily recognize, such as a person or a scene. Mondrian often painted with primary colours and didn't use a ruler to make his lines!

Composition with Large Red Plane, Yellow, Black, Gray and Blue, Piet Mondrian, 1921

You will need

Paper cup

Sharp pencil

String

Safety scissors

Washable paint

Gravity
painting

Gravity is the thing that pulls your feet back to the ground when you jump. Make this splatter paint pendulum to prove that gravity really is there and create amazing abstract art at the same time! It's a bit messy, so work outside.

1

Use a sharp pencil to poke two little holes through the sides of the top of a paper cup. Cut a piece of string, then tie it through the holes.

2

Fill the cup with paint.

3

Poke a little hole in the bottom of the cup.

Large sheet
of paper

4

Lay out a large sheet
of paper, then start
swinging your cup. If it
isn't heavy enough
to swing properly, try
putting some stones
in the cup, too.

Now try...

Add to your design and
make interesting patterns
by changing the colour
of paint in the cup.
Who said art has
to look neat?

What's a pendulum?

A pendulum is something
heavy at the end of a string.
If you push it, it will swing
away from you and then
come back. That's because
gravity is pulling it back to
where it started. Your push
and gravity's pull work
together to make it swing.

Pendulum swinging

Sculptures

Folding

Weaving

Collage

Making

Everything that is human-made has been designed by somebody, including the clothes you wear, the birthday cards you buy, and any sculptures you see. Makers use a mix of materials and tools to craft interesting creations.

Paper craft

Nets

Fashion

Tie-dye

Sculpture

Sculptures are solid, or 3D, works of art that can be made from many different materials. Some are found in art galleries and museums, while others are placed in outdoor public places for everyone to enjoy.

Statues

From ancient Greek and Roman times right up to the present day, statues have been carved to honour gods, warriors, leaders, and other famous people. In Renaissance times, from around 1490–1527, sculptors aimed to produce accurate portrayals of the body. The Renaissance artist Michelangelo was obsessed with making his statues, such as this one on the left, resemble those from ancient Greece and Rome.

David, Michelangelo, 1501-1505. This marble statue is of the Biblical hero David.

Public sculpture

Many cities place sculptures in squares, parks, and gardens. However, you can also find them in more unusual spots such as beaches. Public art is often large and can be viewed from all sides, as with this colourful sculpture by Spanish artist Joan Miró.

Woman and Bird, Joan Miró, 1983

Techniques

Traditionally, sculpture was made using wood or stone, or modelled from clay. When carving hard materials, such as wood, the sculptor chips away with a hammer and chisel. But if the sculptor is using soft clay, then they might mould it using their hands. All sculpture requires patience and precision.

Tools An artist uses particular tools depending on the materials they are working with. Ice sculptures are produced using ice picks, saws, and prongs.

Modern sculpture

Sculptors from the 20th century onwards have become increasingly experimental. They have tried out new techniques and used unusual materials, such as steel, plastic, and glass, to create abstract pieces that spark conversation.

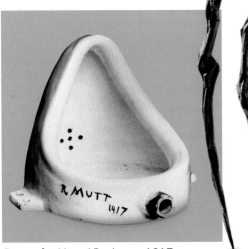

Fountain, Marcel Duchamp, 1917. Duchamp turned everyday objects into "readymade" sculptures, to challenge people to think about what art is and what art could be.

Maman, Louise Bourgeois, 1999. Made from bronze and steel, this huge sculpture's name means "mum" in French. The stupendous spider is more than 9 m (30 ft) high, which is taller than seven eight-year-olds.

Paper crafting

Ever since paper was invented in China more than 2,000 years ago, it's been used to create wonderful crafts. Transform flat, 2D paper into 3D structures, then turn the page to build a paper sculpture.

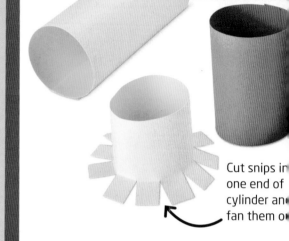

Cut snips in one end of cylinder and fan them out

Rolling

To make a cylinder, roll up a piece of paper so that one end meets the other, and glue them together.

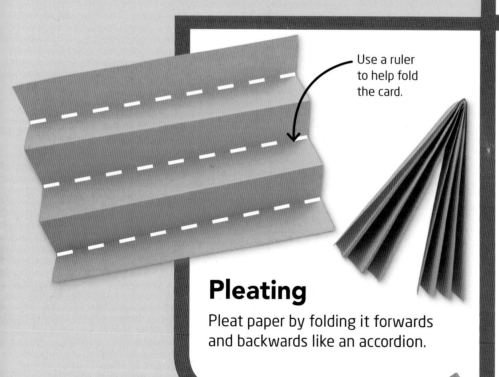

Use a ruler to help fold the card.

Pleating

Pleat paper by folding it forwards and backwards like an accordion.

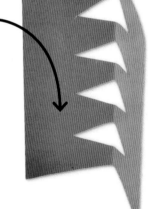

Snip into the crease and then open the paper up to see the effect.

Crease-cutting

Fold paper in half and cut shapes out along the crease.

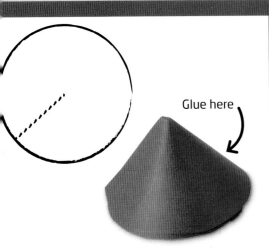

Glue here

Cones

Cut a line into the middle point of a circle. Wrap the circle edge over the remainder of the circle to make a cone.

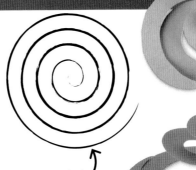

Draw a spiral first and cut along the line.

Spiralling

Cut into the edge of a circle and keep cutting round and round working towards the middle.

Make a grassy effect.

Fringing

Make little snips along a strip of paper without cutting all the way to the other side.

Experiment with tight and loose curled paper by using pencils of different thicknesses.

Curling

Wrap a strip of paper tightly around a pencil to make it curly.

Paper
sculpture

Use the paper engineering techniques you learned on the previous page to create a surreal sculptural landscape. Make your sculpture as interesting as possible by using a variety of paper crafts.

Arrange your sculpture

Gather your paper creations, ensuring that you have a good mix of shapes on different coloured paper, then have fun arranging them!

Can you attach one piece to another without using glue?

Fringing creates height and adds texture to the sculpture.

Experiment with different ways of building up and connecting the different parts of your sculpture.

3D shapes

3D shapes are solid objects. 3D objects can be any shape or size, but these are some common examples.

Cube

Cone

Pyramid

Sphere

Cylinder

Use recycled materials too.

Think about what shapes fit together. This cone sits well on top of the cylinder.

Collage

Almost anything can be used to make a collage. You simply glue paper or material together to make a picture. During his later years, the artist Henri Matisse painted paper in blocks of colour, then cut out shapes to make beautiful collage artworks.

Henri Matisse

French artist Henri Matisse first studied law, but changed his mind after becoming ill and decided to become an artist instead! As a young painter, Matisse was part of the Fauve art movement, whose members were famous for their use of vibrant colours. When he was older, he created many collages.

● **1869–1954**
● **French**

The Sorrows of the King, Henri Matisse, 1952

Glue stick

1 Paint some blocks of colour onto paper and leave them to dry.

2 Draw some shapes onto the back of your painted pieces of paper. Then cut them out.

3 Arrange the shapes on a white or black sheet of paper to make your collage. Think about the composition of your artwork and move the pieces around until you are happy. Finally, glue them in place.

Nōtan design

Artists often use black and white for dramatic effect. Nōtan is an old Japanese design idea, about the balance of light and dark. Use this technique to make your own Nōtan artwork.

1 Use a ruler to draw a 21 x 21 cm (8 x 8 in) square on white paper and cut it out. Then use black paper to draw and cut out a 10 x 10 cm (4 x 4 in) square.

2 Place the black square onto the white paper and draw around it. This will help you return the black square to the same place later.

3 Draw simple shapes from the edge of the black paper and cut them out. Flip the shapes away from the cut out and onto the white paper surrounding it.

Positive and negative space

Positive and negative space are used to draw attention to different aspects of an artwork. The "positive" space is the subject that you want to be the focus of the picture, and the rest of the space is "negative". Look at the two pictures below. What pops out to you? Which colours do you think are the positive and negative spaces?

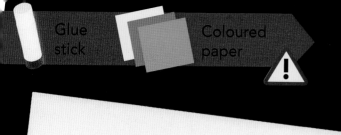
Glue stick

Coloured paper

Now try...
Make a piece of Nōtan artwork using coloured paper. Which effect do you like best?

4
Continue cutting shapes from the black square and flipping them onto the white paper. Once you're happy with the placement of the shapes, you can glue them down.

Be careful not to cut too far into the middle of the black square.

Yin and Yang
This ancient Chinese symbol represents two opposites that need to be balanced to create calm. The black and white opposing sections come together to form a whole circle.

1 Use tracing paper to trace the cube net from pages 134–135 onto paper.

2 With felt-tip pens, doodle a pattern onto one side of the net, then carefully cut it out.

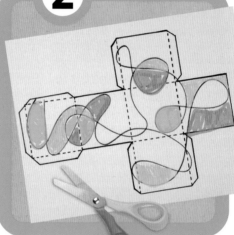

3 Fold along the dotted lines. Put glue on the tabs and stick the shape together.

Doodle cubes

This activity brings art and maths together. A net is a flat 2D shape that can be cut out, folded, and stuck together to make a 3D shape. Decorate cube nets, fold them up, then create a spectacular sculpture tower!

Glue
stick

Create a variety of
different doodle cube
designs, then build a
tower with them!

Cube-inspired art

Artists Georges Braque and Pablo
Picasso begin a movement that would
come to be known as Cubism in the
early 20th century. They explored new
ways of looking at subjects, sometimes
from many angles at the same time.
It was described as reducing art to
"geometric outlines, to cubes".

Modern
example of
Cubist art

Three pipe cleaners

Foil

Masking tape

Cardboard

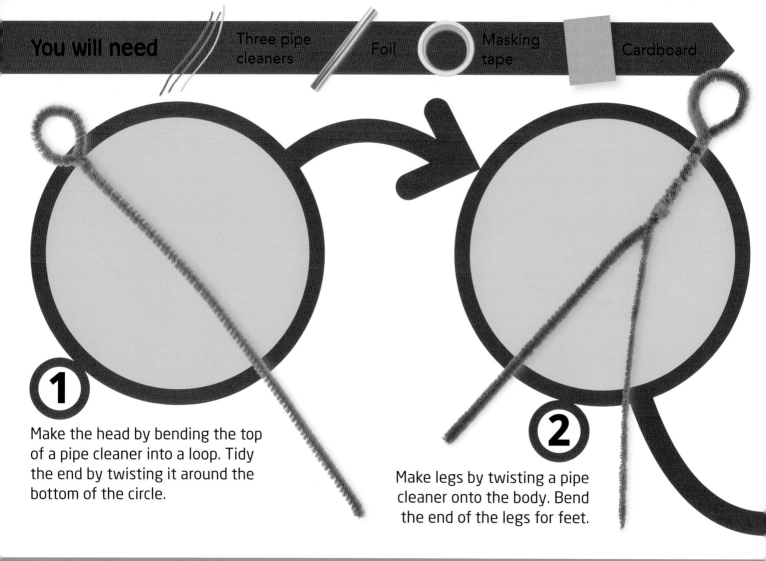

1 Make the head by bending the top of a pipe cleaner into a loop. Tidy the end by twisting it around the bottom of the circle.

2 Make legs by twisting a pipe cleaner onto the body. Bend the end of the legs for feet.

Sculpture figures

This is a fun and simple way to explore making a human form using very few materials. Try making one figure or a family of figures dancing!

Alberto Giacometti

This Swiss artist was fascinated by people and the human form. He moulded many of his sculptures from plaster but some were cast in bronze.

Annette from Life, 1954

Place the last pipe cleaner below the head and then twist each side over and around the body. Loop the ends for hands.

3

Bend the figure into the position you want it to stand, dance, or run. Then tear small lengths of foil and wrap them tightly around the figure.

4

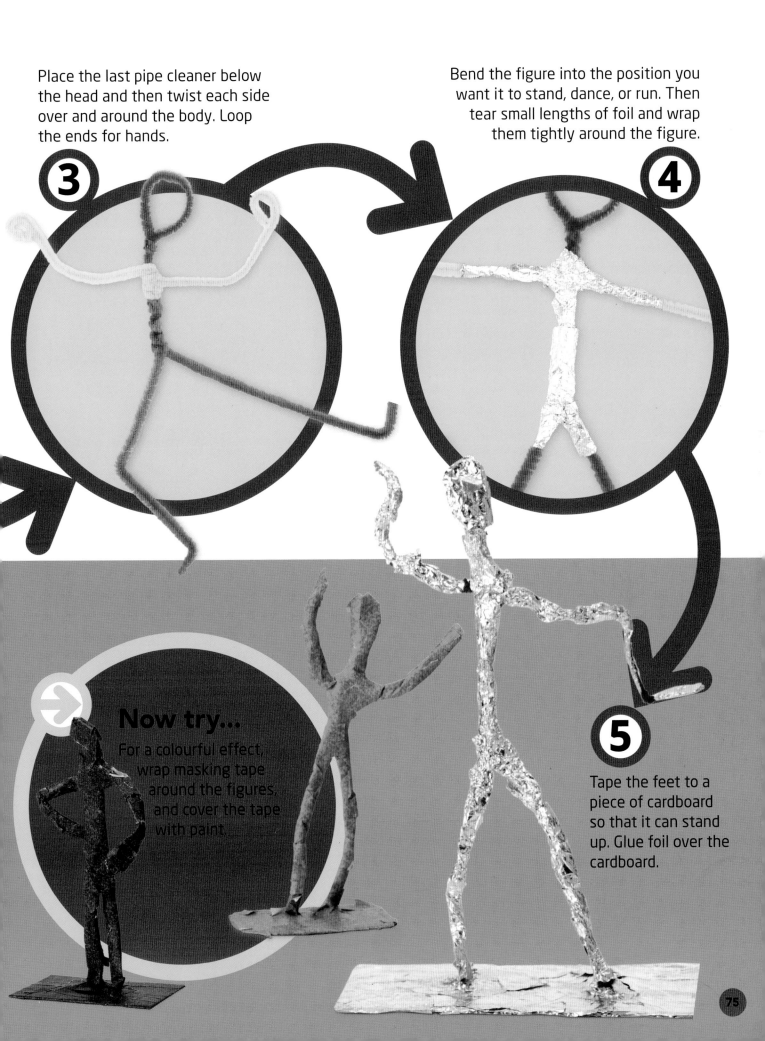

Now try...
For a colourful effect, wrap masking tape around the figures, and cover the tape with paint.

5

Tape the feet to a piece of cardboard so that it can stand up. Glue foil over the cardboard.

Yayoi **Kusama**

Artist • 1929–present • Japanese

Yayoi Kusama is dotty about dots! You can find dots and circles in all of Kusama's wide-ranging work, which includes sculpture, paintings, installations, performance, and fashion pieces.

Mental health

Yayoi Kusama has always used art as a way to express the inner workings of her mind. She has experienced hallucinations since she was a child and has used them to inspire her art. Eventually, Kusama's hallucinations got worse, so in 1977 she moved into a hospital in Japan, where she lives to this day. Kusama has not let this stop her though and she still produces huge amounts of art that's exhibited around the world.

Kusama's childhood hallucinations of spots are what first fuelled her interest in polka dots.

Installations

Art installations often make you feel as if you are being transported to a different world. Kusama welcomed people into her world with The Obliteration Room installation. She painted a room completely white, including the furniture, then invited people to fill the space with colourful, round stickers.

Pumpkin sculptures

Kusama has created many pumpkin sculptures. One of them was installed on Naoshima island, Japan, or "art island" as it is known, at the end of a jetty looking out to sea. It is about 2.2 m (7 ft) tall. Kusama has made her signature dotted pumpkins in many forms, including as huge and tiny sculptures, as well as drawings and paintings.

Pumpkin, Yayoi Kusama, 1994

"Our Earth is only one polka dot among a million stars in the cosmos. Polka dots are a way to infinity."

Kusama is fascinated by pumpkins. She loved drawing kabocha squashes (Japanese pumpkins) as a child on the farm her family owned, and her obsession grew from there.

1

Pour the thickening powder into the water, as instructed on the packet. This will allow the ink to sit on top of the water.

2

Load a pipette or straw with paint, then drip it into the water. Rinse the pipette, reload it with another colour, and repeat the process.

Paper marbling

Here's how to make beautiful marbled paper. Marbling is a great way to experiment with colour and pattern. Each time you do it, the effect is different. When you're finished, use the design as a card for a friend or to cover a book.

3

Make patterns by dragging and swirling a cocktail stick through the water.

4 Hold the paper on either edge so that it dips in the middle a little, then lower it all into the water.

5 Leave for ten seconds, then carefully lift it out and rinse the wet paper under water. Leave it to dry and then you'll have some beautiful paper to use!

Fashion

Fashion designers take influences from around the world to create clothes for us to wear. There are many different styles of fashion, and trends change over the years.

What does a fashion designer do?

A fashion designer creates clothing collections throughout the year. High street or "fast fashion" clothes are made in factories and produced in high quantities. This differs from "haute couture" fashion, which is handmade and very expensive.

Costume design

Costume designers create outfits for special events such as carnivals. They also make outfits worn in TV shows and films.

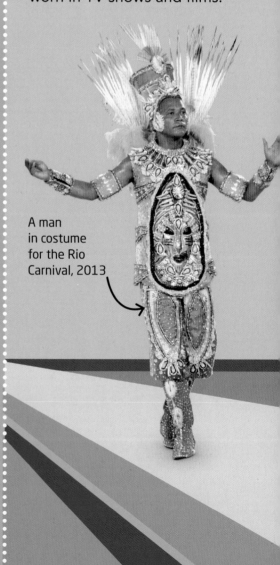

A man in costume for the Rio Carnival, 2013

Coco Chanel

Chanel opened her shop in 1910, and went on to create an empire of clothing, handbags, and jewellery which are still worn today. She made the "LBD" or "little black dress" popular. The House of Chanel still exists and you have to be very talented to work there!

- 1883–1971
- French

Models in Chanel clothing, 1960s

Fashion designers often sketch designs before making them.

Influences on fashion

Fashion can be inspired by anything, from art and architecture to news stories and politics. Celebrities have the power to influence fashion, as their fans often want to dress like them. Many people also care deeply about our planet, and want clothes that have been made in a way that doesn't harm the environment.

Singer Billie Eilish at the Pop Music Awards, 2018

Menswear

Some designers specialize in designing menswear, whether creating a sharp suit or something more unusual.

Changes in fashion

Trends change as often as every few months, but some stick around and become a symbol of an era, such as flared trousers in the 1970s. Ask your parent or caregiver to show you an old photo of them. Do you like the clothes they're wearing? Styles often make comebacks!

A model wearing menswear

Model wearing a summer dress, around 1950

Actress Olivia Newton-John, around 1970

Actress Bai Ling at the Sundance Film Festival, 2002

Tie-dye your clothes

A bunch tied with an elastic band makes a pale ring.

1

Bunch up pieces of your T-shirt and tie elastic bands tightly around each little scrunch.

Wear rubber gloves so that your hands don't get stained.

2

Follow the instructions on the dye packet. Pour the specified amount of water, dye, and salt into the bowl and use a spoon to mix it up. Dunk your T-shirt into the dye and leave it for the time the instructions tell you to wait.

3

Use the spoon to take the T-shirt out and rinse it in cold water, then take off the elastic bands. Hang your T-shirt up to dry and admire your fun new top!

Rubber gloves   Bowl of water

Create a cool new look by tie-dyeing an old T-shirt! The secret to tie-dyeing is elastic bands – the dye doesn't stain the area that the band covers. Wear gloves and cover surfaces so that you don't stain anything, or do it outside.

Make a circular pattern like this by tying an elastic band onto the centre of a T-shirt. Add more bands around it, with a little space between each one.

Use masking tape to attach fabric onto a piece of card. This will keep it still.

1

2 For the parts of your design that you want to stay white, draw a pattern onto the fabric in glue. Leave to dry.

Glue
batik

Batik is an ancient art form that uses wax or glue to create patterns on fabric. First, draw a picture with glue, then cover it with dye or paint. Finally, scrape off the glue to reveal the design. This technique is known as "resist dyeing".

Mix your paints with water and apply to the fabric. When the paint is completely dry, peel off the cardboard backing. Place the fabric in warm water to loosen the glue, then scrape it off.

3

You can use a nail brush to help scrub off the glue.

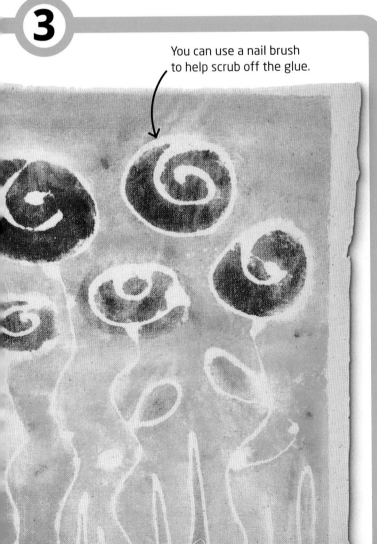

Batik around the world

The word "batik" is thought to come from the Javanese words *amba*, meaning "to write", and *titik*, which means "dot". Batik originates from Java, Indonesia, but the method is now widely used by people in countries across Asia and Africa.

Malaysian batik

Indonesian batik

African patchwork batik

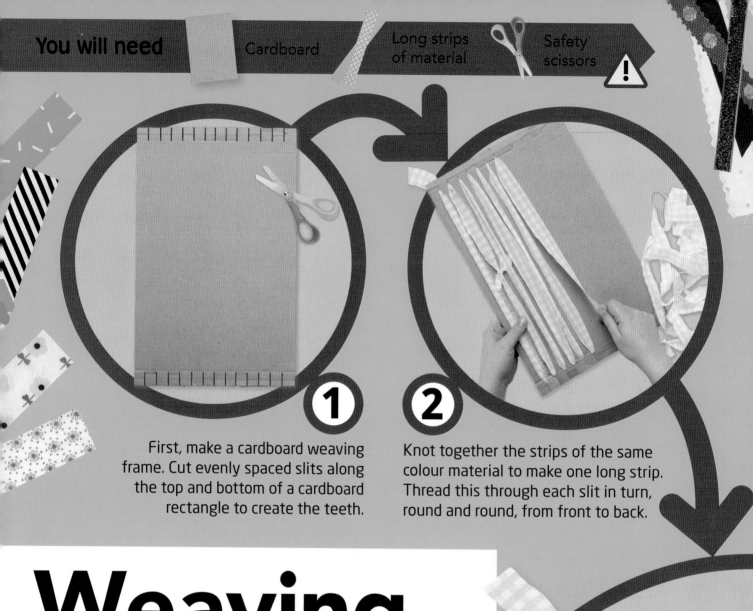

1

First, make a cardboard weaving frame. Cut evenly spaced slits along the top and bottom of a cardboard rectangle to create the teeth.

2

Knot together the strips of the same colour material to make one long strip. Thread this through each slit in turn, round and round, from front to back.

Weaving

The wonderful craft of weaving has been practised for centuries. People weave to make clothes, baskets, fences, mats, and more. Some cultures still weave by hand, but a lot of weaving is now performed by big machines.

3

Weave strips of another colour over and under the vertical strips.

Use strips of whatever materials you can find. It's a great way to recycle unwanted scraps.

Ribbons

Plastic bags

Old fabric

4 When you've filled the frame, turn the board over and snip through the fabric strips. Pull your creation off the board.

5 Knot pairs of strips at the end of the weave together and cut them to the same length.

Pull the strip all the way through before starting the next line. When a piece of fabric runs out, knot another strip onto the end and carry on weaving.

Warp and weft

The under-and-over method of weaving is referred to as "warp and weft". The warp lines are the vertical lines of fabric going down the frame, and the weft lines are the horizontal lines.

A Peruvian woman weaving

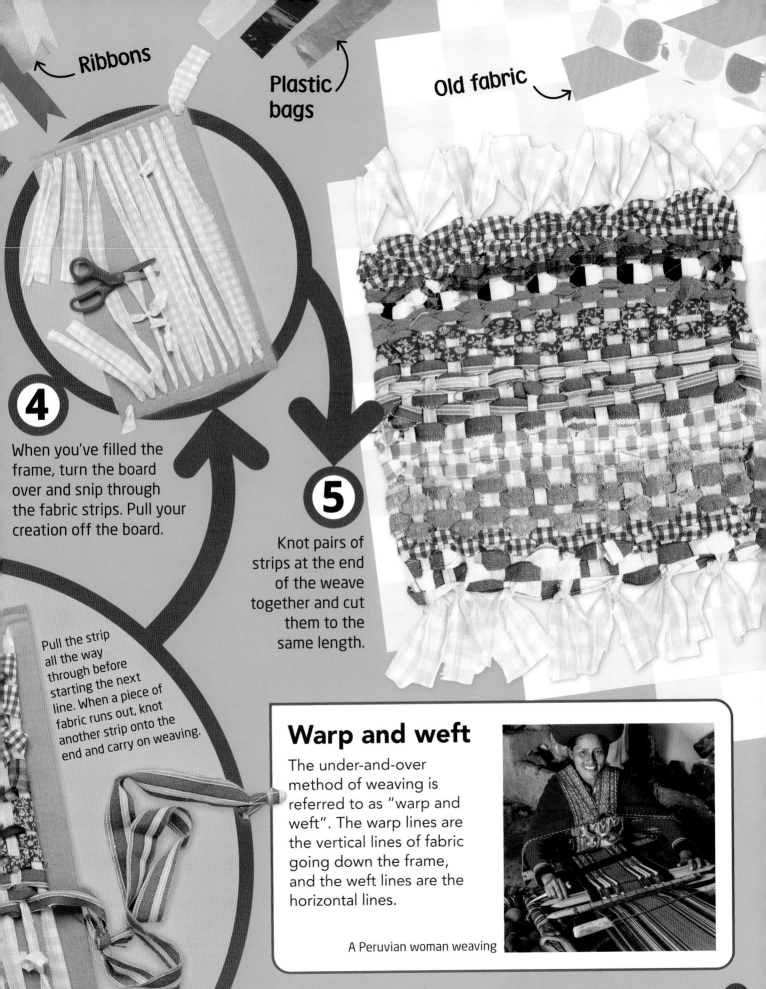

Environment

Camouflage

Golden ratio

Nature

The natural world is full of inspiration. Some artists create installations outside, or use natural materials in their work. How does nature inspire you? It might be the light on a summer's day or the symmetry of a flower.

Sunprints

Inspiration

Symmetry

Landscapes

Leaf patterns

Sahara Desert Rock Art, around 12,000 BCE

Nature in prehistoric art

Ancient cave paintings show us that animals and nature were very important to ancient humans. The art often shows animals that were alive at the time.

Colours from nature

There were no art supplies thousands of years ago. Instead, people used materials they found in nature to draw and add colour.

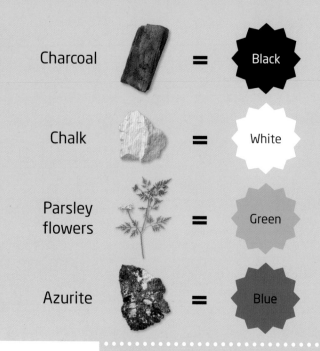

Charcoal = Black

Chalk = White

Parsley flowers = Green

Azurite = Blue

Natural beauty

From prehistoric times through to the modern day, artists have always found inspiration in nature. Whether it's an animal, the changing seasons, or a beautiful landscape, there is much about nature that is artful.

Vinicunca, or Rainbow Mountain, in Cusco Region, Peru

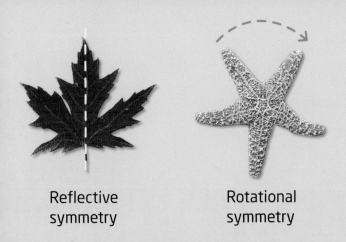

Reflective symmetry

Rotational symmetry

Symmetry in nature

Symmetry is pleasing to the eye. Nature has many examples of reflective symmetry, which is when different sides of an object look the same. This is often visible in flowers and leaves. A starfish shows rotational symmetry – when an object can be turned around until it fits exactly into its original outline. Can you think of anything else that is symmetrical in this way?

The golden ratio

The "golden ratio" is a mathematical equation that describes proportions, and it turns up in all sorts of places in nature, such as the spiral of this shell. Pictures with shapes that fit into the golden ratio look balanced and appealing. Many artists, including Leonardo da Vinci, have used it in their art.

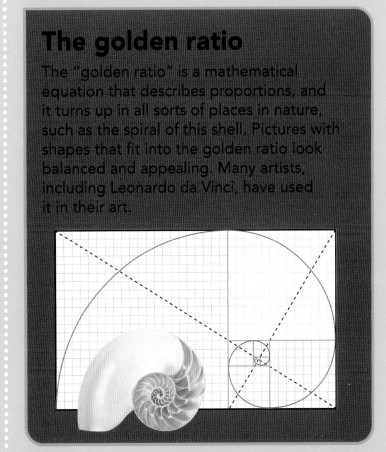

This landscape looks as if it has been painted, but it's completely natural. The colours are from the minerals in the rocks.

Landscape painting

Landscape art was being made as early as the 4th century in China. Landscape painting became popular in Western art during the Romantic period (1800–1850), with artists such as John Constable creating atmospheric scenes.

Hampstead Heath with a Rainbow, John Constable, 1836

Andy Goldsworthy

Land artist and photographer • 1956-present • British

Andy Goldsworthy is a land artist. This means he uses natural materials such as stone, branches, and leaves to create his art, which he often displays in a natural setting. Many of his works don't last for very long, crumbling away or melting down.

Midsummer Snowballs, 2000

The passing of time

Much of Goldsworthy's work is about how things alter over time. This is reflected in the materials he uses, which often naturally change form, such as snow. "It's not about art," he has explained. "It's just about life and the need to understand that a lot of things in life do not last."

Materials

Goldsworthy uses natural materials that he finds at his chosen location for the tools as well as the art. He forms the natural objects into the shape of something else found in nature, such as this leaf sculpture formed into a pine cone shape.

Leaves

Stones

The artistic process

Goldsworthy follows a routine each time he works on a project. First he selects a location, then he gathers his natural materials and tools. Next he creates his sculpture and takes a photograph of the work. Finally he leaves his art to the elements. He finds it very interesting to see what happens to it afterwards.

Andy combined natural elements, such as sticks, to create a sculpture that looks like a spider's web.

"Each work grows, stays, decays..."

Drumlanrig Sweet Chestnut, 1989

Even ice!

Nature patterns

Making patterns with natural materials is a great way of connecting with nature. You can make an unlimited number of designs by arranging different objects, found in a park, a garden, or the beach.

2 Starting from the centre and working outwards, arrange your materials in a circle. Try using repeating patterns to make a design.

1 Collect a few different types of objects - fallen leaves or petals are ideal. Make sure you don't disturb any creepy-crawlies!

Miniature models

In the late 1800s, there was a trend for arranging diatoms – tiny single-celled organisms with delicate glass skeletons. Artists used microscopes to create beautiful miniature designs with them. Today, a German artist called Klaus Kemp carries on this tradition, making minute diatom artworks that can be less than 1 mm (0.04 in) in size. That's smaller than a grain of rice!

Diatom pattern by Klaus Kemp, 2016

3

Take a photo of your creation to remember it, then leave it outdoors.

There are lots of repeating patterns in nature – such as the seeds in a sunflower.

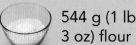

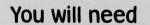

Combine the flour and salt in a bowl. Add the water little by little, stirring all the time.

2

Knead the dough together until a smooth dough forms.

3

1

Gather some natural materials together. Items with a clear outline such as leaves or flowers work best.

Hanging sculptures

Try making these delicate hanging sculptures! They are made by pressing flowers and plants into salt dough. Once ready, the nature sculptures can hang inside or outside your home.

4

Roll out the dough with a rolling pin and make some shapes with a cookie cutter.

237 ml (8 fl oz) water	Rolling pin	Baking paper	Baking tray	Pencil

Now try...

Paint your sculptures for a more dreamy, arty feel!

Pull pieces of ribbon or string through the holes. Your hanging sculptures will now be ready to hang wherever you wish!

7

Use a pencil to make the holes.

5

Press the natural items into the dough.

6

Preheat an oven to 135ºC (275ºF). Use a pencil to make a hole in the top of each shape and place on a lined baking tray. Bake for 2 hours. Take out and leave to cool.

Line the tray with baking paper.

To make the frame, draw a square onto your card and carefully cut it out. You might need an adult to help with this.

Then cut out two squares of sticky-back plastic. Fix one piece onto the back of the frame.

Carefully arrange the natural items on the sticky surface.

1 **2** **3**

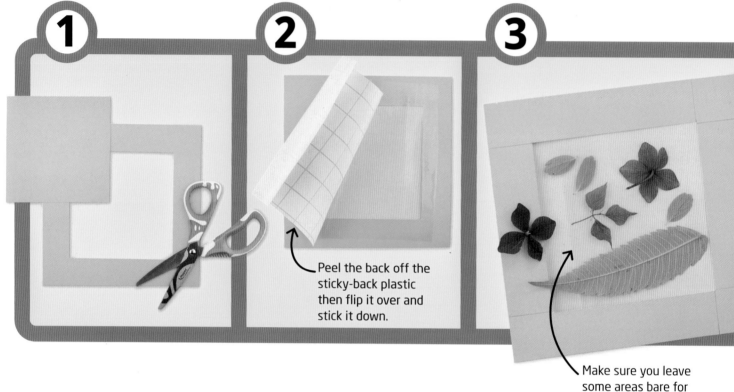

Peel the back off the sticky-back plastic then flip it over and stick it down.

Make sure you leave some areas bare for the light to shine through.

Window
wonders

Bring the outdoors inside with these simple sun catchers that are made using natural items. Even on a cloudy day these colourful decorations will cheer up your room.

Make the frames in different colours!

Natural items

Hole punch

Ribbon

Stick the other square of sticky-back plastic over the top of the natural items so they're sandwiched between the two sheets.

4

5

Make a hole in the frame using a hole punch. Then thread some ribbon through it so you can hang your creation up.

Pin a piece of light-sensitive paper to cardboard and lay it outside. Quickly arrange the natural items, in this case feathers, on the paper. Wait a few minutes.

1

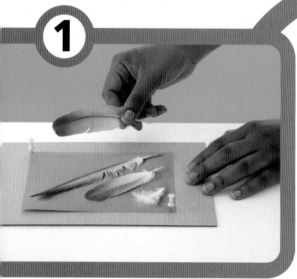

2

The paper will change colour from deep to pale blue. Then remove the feathers and unpin the paper. You'll see shadows where the feathers stopped the sunlight from reaching the paper.

Sun prints

This arty experiment produces incredible results while revealing a lot about how sunshine and shadows work. You need some special light-sensitive paper, which you can get from craft stores or online. This activity works best on a sunny day.

3 Place the paper into a tray of water. The deep blue colour of the feathers will wash off, and the pale blue areas will turn darker blue. Leave the paper in the water for a few minutes.

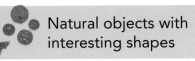

Dry the paper by placing it inside a folded tea towel. Put a heavy object, such as a book, on top of the towel for a few hours. This will keep it flat and let it dry off.

4

How it works

Light-sensitive paper is coated in chemicals that react together when they are exposed to a type of light called ultraviolet. This reaction causes a deep-blue colour to form on the paper. When the paper is put in water, the original chemicals – which remain in areas that sunlight hasn't reached – wash away, but the deep-blue colouring remains.

5 Unfold the tea towel to check the paper. If it's dry, your print is ready! See how the paper has changed colour yet again - the blue areas are much darker now, so the white feather prints really stand out.

Try using leaves too.

Make a frame from card so that your print really stands out.

Clever camouflage

Camouflage is a pattern or colouring that allows an animal or object to blend into the background. Some animals, such as chameleons, are well camouflaged in their environment.

2 Trace the chameleon template from pages 134–135 and cut it out. Colour it in the same way you coloured the background, but use smaller shapes.

1 Create a background by drawing shapes onto paper. Fill them in using similar coloured crayons such as orange and yellow.

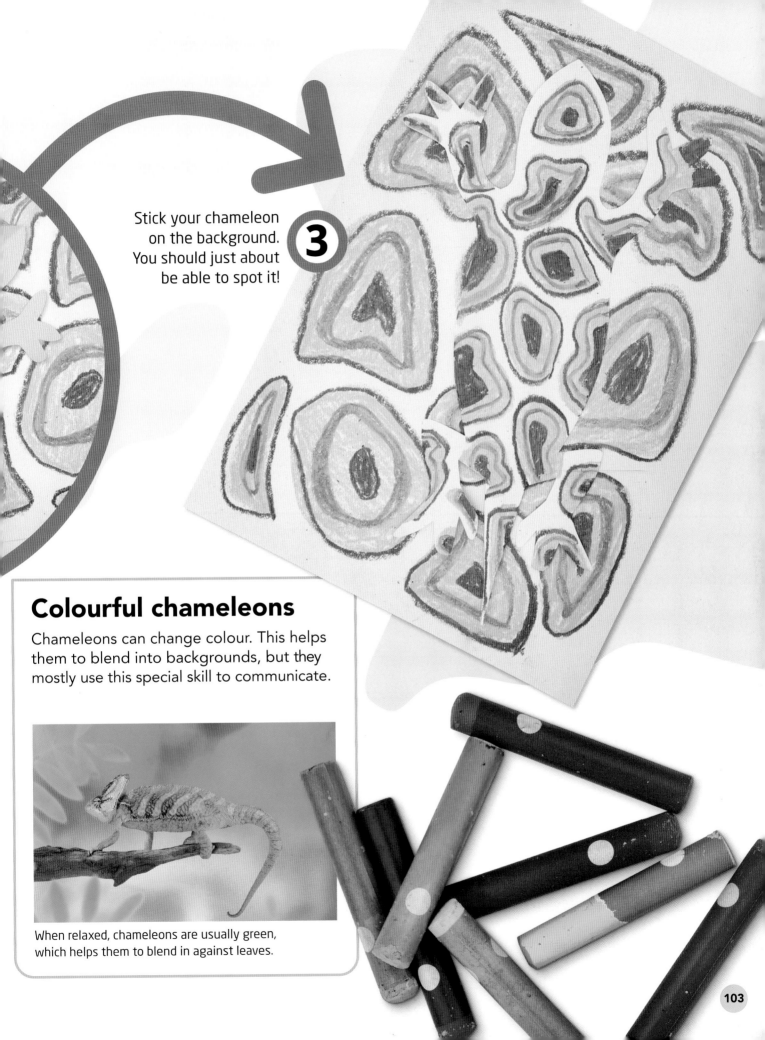

Stick your chameleon
on the background.
You should just about
be able to spot it!

3

Colourful chameleons

Chameleons can change colour. This helps
them to blend into backgrounds, but they
mostly use this special skill to communicate.

When relaxed, chameleons are usually green,
which helps them to blend in against leaves.

Set design

Zoetrope

Characters

Film reel

Photography and animation

Before we had cameras and film, people produced moving pictures using shadow puppets and spinning toys. Advances in technology have led to many new ways of producing digital art, including photography and computer animation.

Stop motion

Movies

Projections

Digital art

Frames

Photography

The word photography means "drawing with light". A photograph is a recording of what the eye can see, but different effects can make the image stand out. As well as cameras, most phones and tablets take photographs - so anyone can be a photographer!

First photograph

A French inventor named Joseph Niépce captured some of the first photographs, including this view from his window in Burgundy, France. Early photographs took days to create.

View from the Window at Le Gras, Joseph Niépce, around 1826

Landscape

Striking landscapes are popular subjects for photographers. This autumn landscape invites the viewer into the scene to look at the interesting view. The striking colour of the trees gives the viewer something to focus on. This is known as the focal point.

Two fiery-throated Hummingbirds, Savegre, Costa Rica

Wildlife

Photographers of wildlife have to be quick to get their shot, and lucky too. Some nature photographers wait for weeks to get the image they want. They often use long lenses on their cameras to zoom in on animals in their natural environment .

A mountain landscape, Sokilsky ridge, Ukraine

Photoshoots

Photographers rarely just take one photograph at a time. They may have to take thousands to get the perfect shot. They often set up a space to have photoshoots, where they bring equipment including bright lights, and sometimes an assistant to help.

Behind the scenes of a photoshoot

Fashion

Fashion photography is incredibly creative. The images can have strong themes to help show off new pieces of clothing. Backgrounds, jewellery, and make-up all contribute to the overall look of the photograph.

A woman modelling a dress

Portrait of Sharbat Gula, Steve McCurry, 1984

Photojournalism

Photojournalists are photographers who use images to report on news events, such as wars. They usually have to travel all over the world. The photographs they take often tell a whole story in just a single image.

Cameras through history

Early cameras could only take one image at a time. The invention of camera film allowed multiple images to be taken. With digital cameras, we can now shoot an almost unlimited number of photos.

1839
Alphonse Giroux sold a "daguerreotype" camera that took single images.

1888
George Eastman invented the Kodak, which came with film inside and could take 100 pictures.

1913
The Leica, created by Oskar Barnack, was smaller and easier to carry around.

1948
The first Polaroid camera not only took a picture but also printed it at the same time.

1975
Digital cameras began to replace film cameras. They became smaller and more powerful over time.

Present day
Today, digital cameras are built into many devices. Most phones can now take high-quality pictures.

107

Gerda Taro

War photographer • 1910-1937 • From Germany

As a young Jewish woman living in Nazi Germany, Gerda Taro had a strong sense of right and wrong. She became a photojournalist, and took pictures of the Spanish Civil War. Today, Gerda is recognized as a pioneer in war photography.

Art activist

Gerda made her opposition to the Nazis clear and in 1933 she was captured by them. Luckily she was released and fled to Paris, but she never saw her family again. In Paris, Gerda met photographer Endre Friedmann, who saw that Gerda had a talent for taking pictures too. They fell in love and began working together. Tragically, while taking photographs during the Spanish Civil War, Gerda was struck by a tank and killed.

Gerda's photographs were developed from rolls of film.

Gerta Pohorylle

Gerda Taro

Gerda's original surname was Gerta Pohorylle, but she changed it to disguise the fact that she was Jewish.

Photojournalism

Photojournalists are always on the lookout for that special shot that captures a single moment or reflects a mood. Gerda took this picture at the start of the Spanish Civil War in 1936. It shows two boys in Barcelona on a barricade, set up to protect against opposing forces.

Gerda used dynamic camera angles - holding the camera high above her head helped her get aerial shots of the frontline in war.

Gerda and Endre

Like Gerda, Endre had also fled from the Nazis in Germany. After they teamed up in Paris, they invented an imaginary person called Robert Capa - supposedly an American photographer - and sold photographs under that name.

The Mexican Suitcase

Three cardboard boxes full of more than 4,000 film negatives were found in Mexico City in 1994. The collection, known as The Mexican Suitcase, revealed pictures taken during the Spanish Civil War by Gerda and Endre, as well as another by a photographer named David Seymour.

The Mexican Suitcase, on display in a museum

Movie-maker

Become a movie-maker with this amazing moving picture activity. First, draw separate scenes and characters. Then use your home-made movie to scroll through the different pictures and make up a story as you go!

1

Open and flatten out the cardboard box. Draw a small rectangle for the screen, then draw around the end of a cardboard roll four times, in the positions below.

Carefully cut out all the holes. You can push a pencil through the cardboard into a piece of sticky tack on the other side to safely make a hole, then cut into it with scissors.

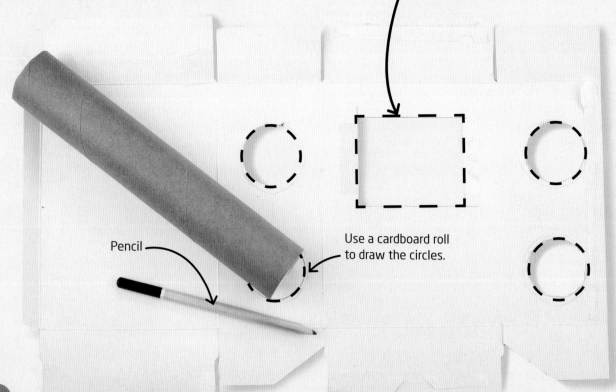

Pencil

Use a cardboard roll to draw the circles.

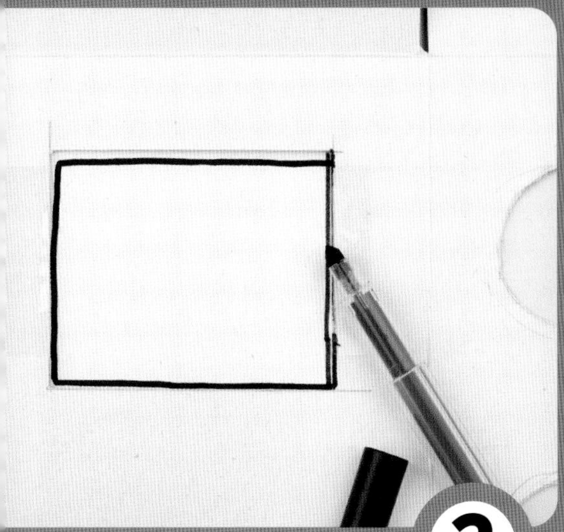

2

Use the window you've cut out as a stencil to draw a film reel strip. Draw four or five of these rectangles onto a strip of paper, then have fun drawing colourful designs in each one!

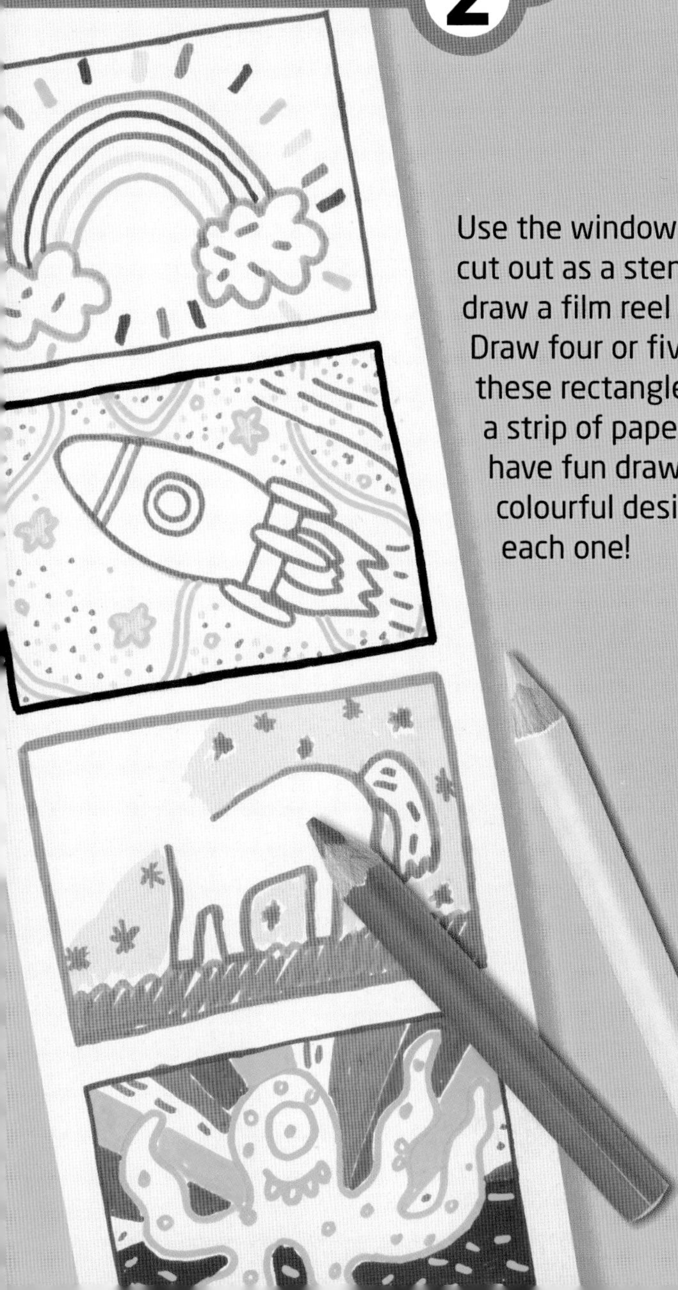

Loop three elastic bands onto the middle of a cardboard roll, then push it through the top-right hole of the box. Fix the top-left hole onto the other side of the roll. Then slot the other cardboard roll through the second set of holes.

3

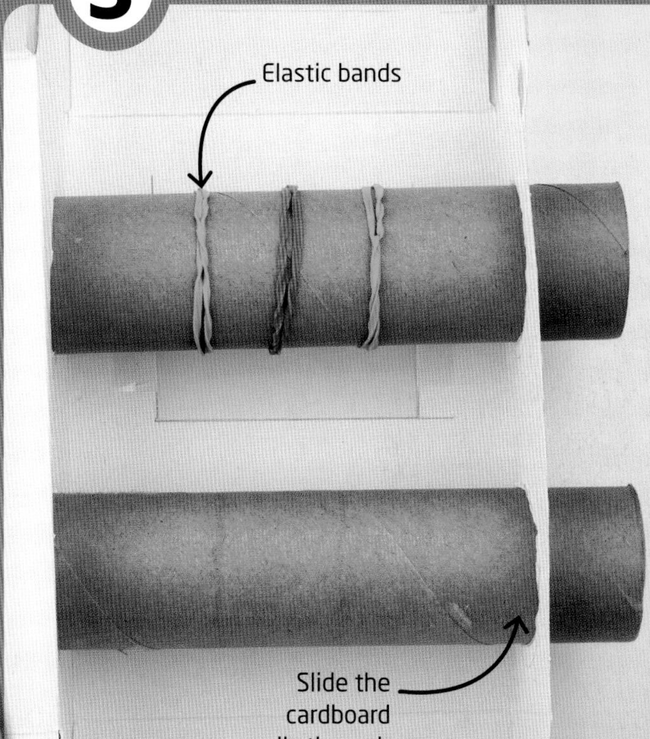

Elastic bands

Slide the cardboard rolls through the holes.

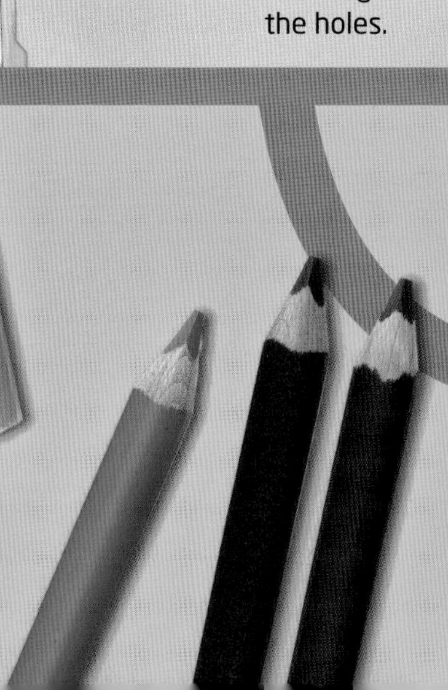

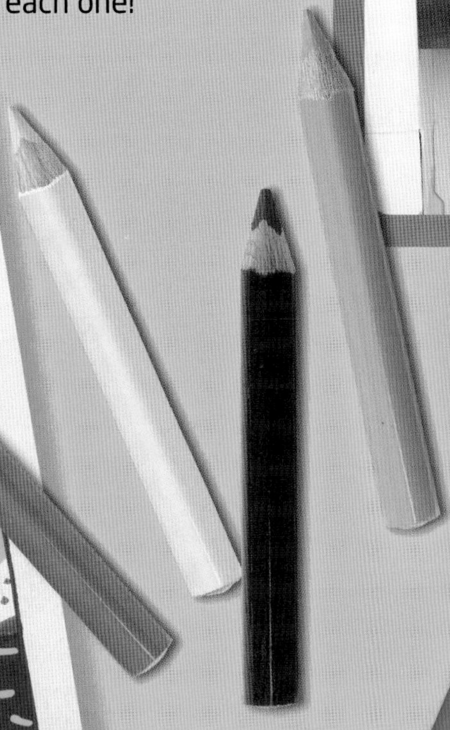

Use sticky tape to attach the
top of the picture strip to the
top cardboard roll. Then stick
the other end of the strip
to the bottom roll.

5

Stick the edge of
the picture reel onto
the cardboard rolls
as shown here.

Fold the top of the box
over and seal it on one
side with sticky tape.

6

Turn here

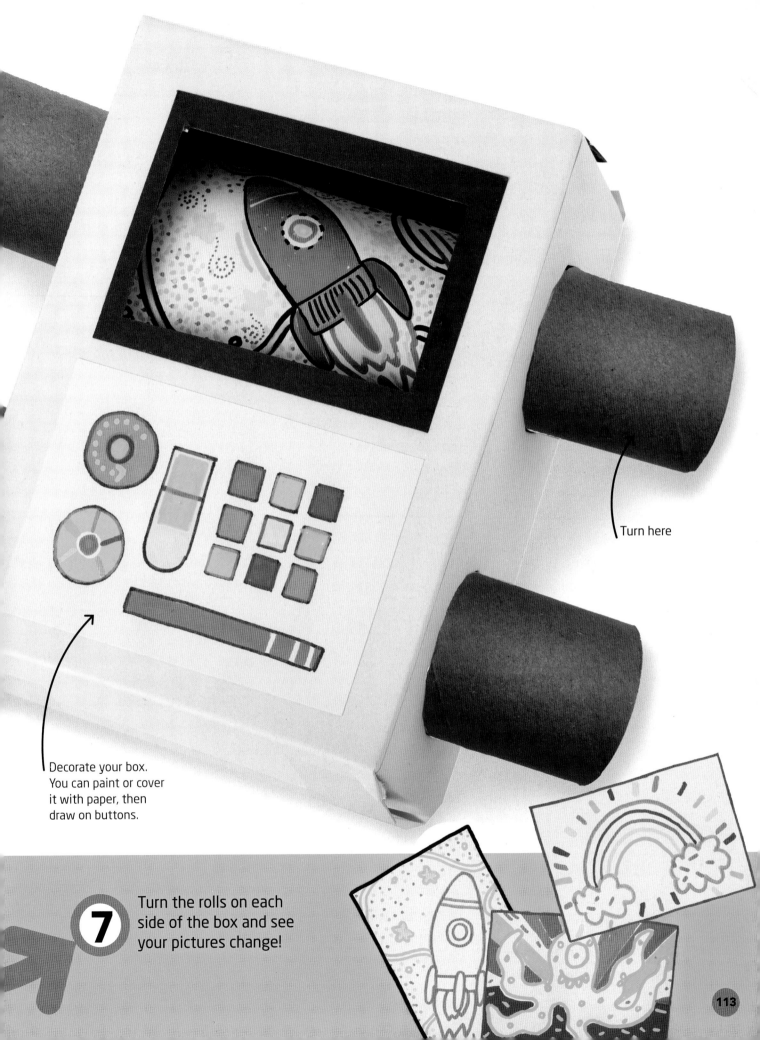

Turn here

Decorate your box. You can paint or cover it with paper, then draw on buttons.

7 Turn the rolls on each side of the box and see your pictures change!

You will need | Stack of sticky notes | Felt-tip

What to draw?

Choose a simple drawing, such as a stick person waving, a car moving, or a ball bouncing. Then draw the image over and over on each page with slight changes to it; this is what will make it appear to move when you flip the pages.

Flipbook

Flipbooks are a great introduction to the moving image world of animation, as they're like little hand-held films. By making small changes to each drawing, your pictures will appear to move!

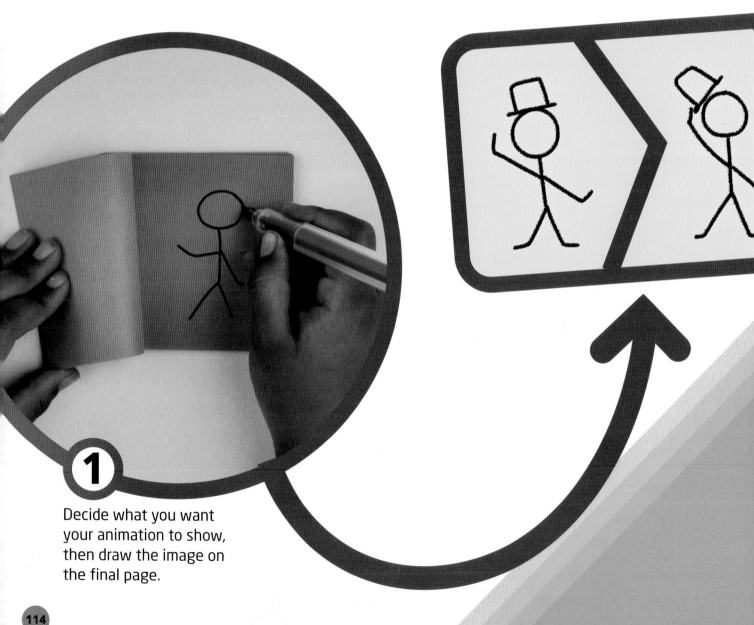

1

Decide what you want your animation to show, then draw the image on the final page.

2

Carefully sketch the drawing for each page, making only a slight change to it each time.

3

When you have finished, flip the pages to watch your animation come to life!

Hayao Miyazaki

Animator and filmmaker • 1941-present • Japanese

As a child, **Hayao Miyazaki** loved to draw, and he also had an interest in animation and comics. He studied politics and economics at university, but after he graduated Miyazaki returned to his first love - drawing - and began working as an animator.

Early animation

When he was growing up in Japan, Miyazaki was always interested in storytelling, especially through animation. He believed traditional art skills were important, so he drew many of his early films entirely by hand. Today, many animated films are made using computer graphics or digital drawings instead of hand-drawn illustrations.

Hayao Miyazaki and Isao Takahata, another director at Studio Ghibli

My Neighbour Totoro, 1988

Studio Ghibli

In 1985, Miyazaki got together with some friends to open an animation studio. They called it "Studio Ghibli", and their movies are popular with children and adults alike. Studio Ghibli has won many awards over the years, including an Oscar for *Spirited Away*. There is even a Ghibli museum in Tokyo, Japan, and plans to build a Ghibli theme park near Nagoya, Japan.

"Always believe in yourself. Do this and no matter where you are, you will have nothing to fear."

Aeroplanes

Miyazaki was born during World War II. His family had to evacuate twice, and one city where they lived was bombed. His father ran a company that made rudders for fighter planes. Miyazaki was greatly affected by these experiences, and planes feature in many of his films, such as *Porco Rosso* and *The Wind Rises*.

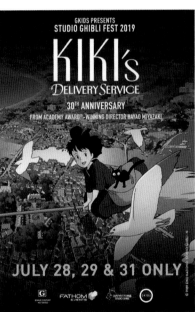

Porco Rosso planes were the influence for Miyazaki's 1992 film *Porco Rosso.*

Themes

Studio Ghibli films often follow similar themes. Many of the movies focus on the difference between the real and spiritual world, or the power and importance of nature. Most also have a strong female lead character.

Card

 Safety scissors

 Lamp

Phone or tablet with stop-motion app

Stop motion

This is an amazing way to make your own short film. It takes practice, and you need lots of patience, but it's worth the effort!

Preparation

Make sure you have everything you need before you start your stop-motion film.

Backdrop
You can draw your own background, or reuse wrapping paper, fabric, or even a pillowcase!

Lighting
Remember that the lighting needs to be the same in each frame, or photograph. Natural light changes throughout the day, so it may be better to use a lamp.

Filming
The smaller the movement your subject makes, the more realistic the animation will be. Small details are key. Each set-up scene is called a "frame". Real animated films usually have 24 frames in a single second!

1

Set up your scene and take a photo. Then change one thing, such as adding another cloud, and take another photograph.

Add in the different parts of the flower, one part at a time.

3

2 Add a flower stem to the scene using moulded plasticine. Make it look like the flower is growing by making it a little taller in each frame.

4 See the finished effect by scrolling through your photos quickly, or upload the images to a stop-motion app.

Make a tiger marionette

This string puppet activity is a great way to recycle cardboard rolls. Once you've made your tiger, use the strings to make it dance! Then create more marionette animals to put on a puppet show.

1 Cover orange paper in glue and stick it onto the cardboard roll. Then cut another cardboard roll in half for the tiger's head, and cover this in orange paper too.

Fringe the edges and push them inside the roll.

2 Use a black felt-tip to draw tiger stripes on the big tube. Draw a face on the smaller tube.

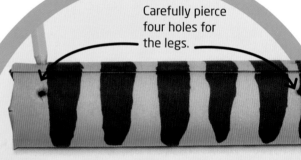

Carefully pierce four holes for the legs.

3 Push a sharp pencil into the underside of the long tube to make space for four legs. Then pierce one hole at the back of the head tube, and another on top of the body, at the tail end.

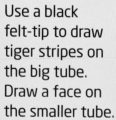

4 Make legs by threading a 30 cm (12 in) piece of ribbon through the two front holes under the body and leave them dangling. Repeat this with the two holes on the other end of the tube.

Attach a folded tail to the end of the body.

You can also cut out, decorate, and stick on little ears.

To attach the body to the head, thread ribbon through the hole on top of the body and pull it through the whole tube to the opening at the head end. Then push it through the hole in the back of the head.

5

Thread the ribbon through the two holes.

Add detail to the face.

Use the black felt-tip to draw feet.

6 Cross two lolly sticks and tie ribbon around the middle. Then attach this ribbon to the ribbon that has been threaded through the tiger's body and head. Now you can start making your puppet move!

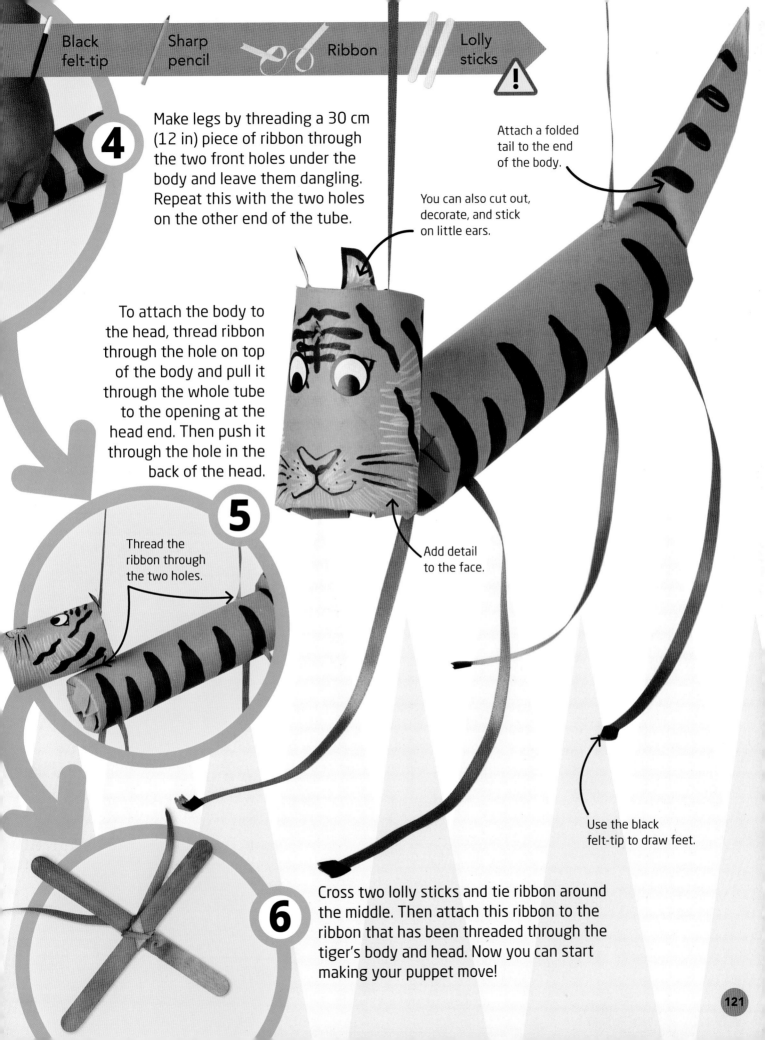

121

Puppet show

Put on a show with your very own puppet theatre! First, pick a theme and decide what characters and scenery you need - we've chosen to set our show in a jungle. Then create your theatre. Finish off by putting on a performance for your friends!

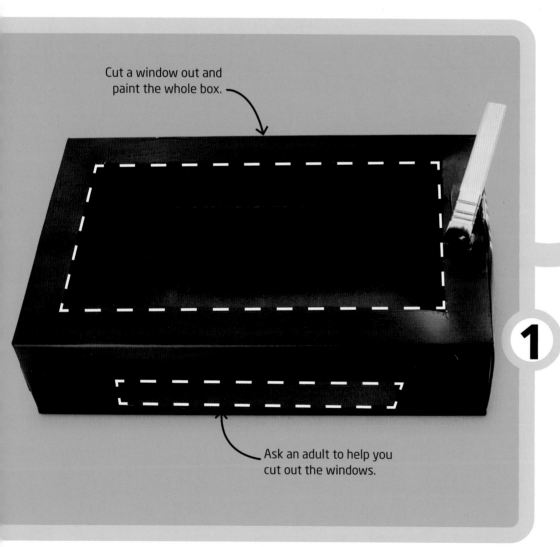

Cut a window out and paint the whole box.

Ask an adult to help you cut out the windows.

1 Cut a rectangular window out of the front of your box, and then a smaller rectangle along one of the sides. Then paint your box black and leave it to dry.

 Coloured card

 Felt-tips

 Straws

 Sticky tape

You can add detail to the scene using felt-tips.

2

Pick a scene you would like to make for the set. Choose a piece of coloured card to stick at the back of your box. This will be the background. Paint a more detailed layer of scenery to go in front of the background.

Create several more layers of scenery.

3

Make grass scenery by painting a piece of card green, then snipping little triangles into the top edge.

Repeat this with another piece of card, then fold in one edge in so that it can stand up.

You can also cut out little leaves and stick them onto the box to decorate it.

Arrange the scenery inside the box in any way you like.

4

7

Now it's time to put on a show! Slide the puppets through the slit in the top of the box and hold the straws to move your characters around the set.

5

Now make the characters. Use a pencil to draw their outlines on card, then cut them out and decorate!

Tape the characters to the end of the straws.

No theatre is complete without red curtains! Fold a piece of red card in half, then draw half an hourglass shape. Cut this out and you will have two curtains. Stick them to the inside of the box, on either side of the stage.

6

Fold your card to make it pleated.

Cut along the hourglass outline.

Folded card

Pleating makes the card look more like real theatre curtains!

Rehearse your play first, then perform it in front of an audience!

What are your characters called?

Paper spinner

Make these super spinners to create optical illusions. Two images will look like they've magically merged when you spin them quickly!

Your two circles must be the same size.

1

Draw and cut out two circles. Draw a flower low down on one and a butterfly high up on the other one.

2

Put glue on the back of the circles and stick them back to back, with the pencil in between them.

Stick the circles onto the end of the pencil.

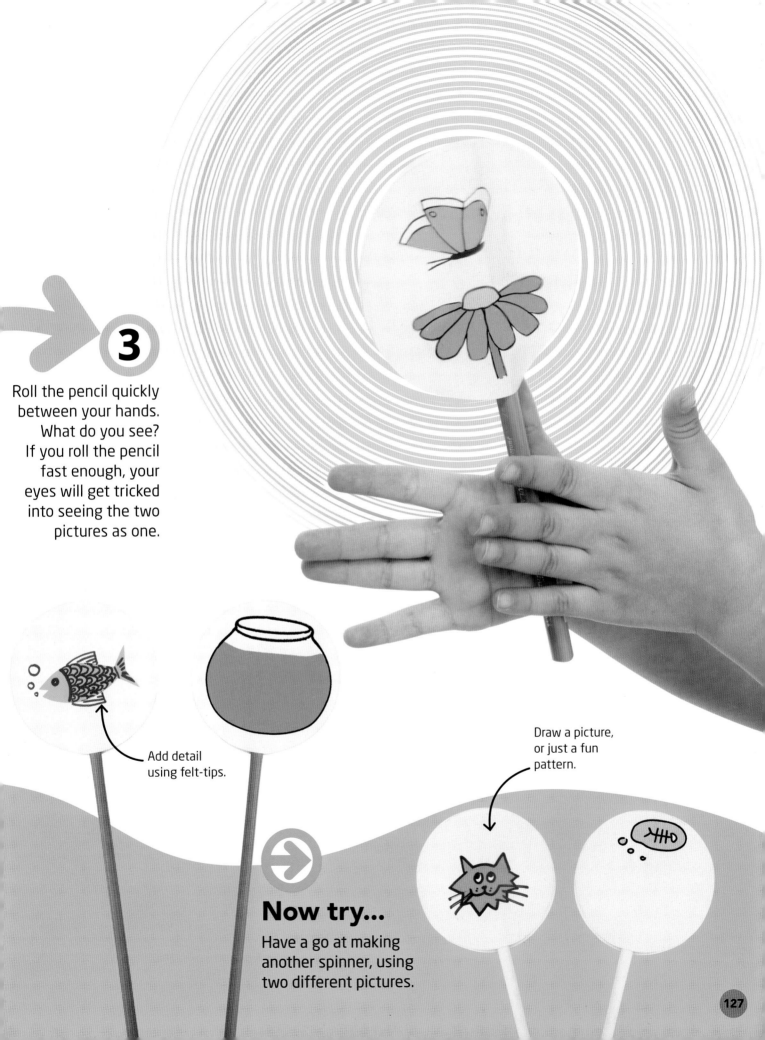

3

Roll the pencil quickly between your hands. What do you see? If you roll the pencil fast enough, your eyes will get tricked into seeing the two pictures as one.

Add detail using felt-tips.

Draw a picture, or just a fun pattern.

Now try...

Have a go at making another spinner, using two different pictures.

Zoetrope

Every film or television programme you have ever watched is a series of pictures sped up. Your brain fills in the gaps between the pictures and sees movement. A zoetrope was an early way of achieving this.

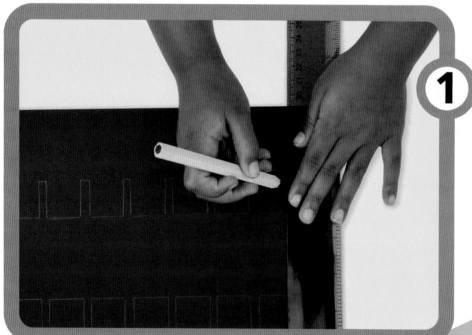

1 To make the outer part of the zoetrope, trace the template from pages 134–135 onto dark paper and cut it out. Use a ruler to help draw straight lines.

Black pen | Paper plate | Sticky tack

History of the zoetrope

Zoetropes were popular toys in the 19th century. William George Horner invented the modern zoetrope in 1834. It was a slotted cylinder lined with images. As it spun around, each picture was seen for a fraction of a second through a slot. If it spun fast enough, the pictures merged together and appeared to move.

Cut the shape out and tape it together to make a cylindrical shape.

2

Cut a strip of white paper that, when curved, fits snugly inside the black cylinder, no taller than the slits. Draw a series of simple images, such as a stick person in slightly different poses, along the strip. Curve the strip and tape it together into a loop.

3

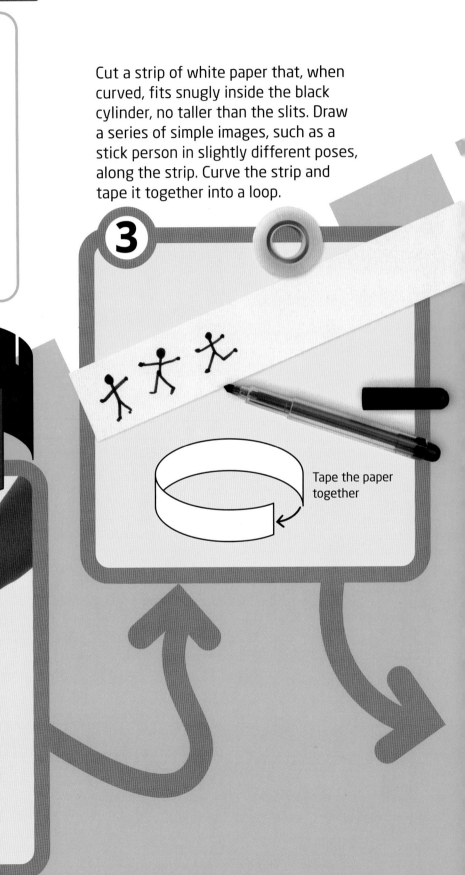

Tape the paper together

Fix tape to the bottom of the black paper loop and stick this onto the paper plate. Then slip the white loop of paper inside the black.

5

Find the centre of the paper plate and push a pencil through it. Press some sticky tack around the pencil to hold it in place.

4

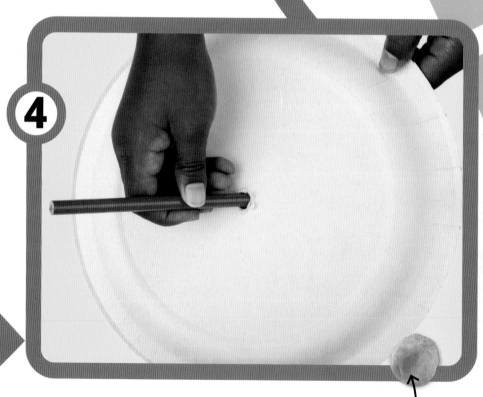

Turn to page 8 to find out how to use sticky tack to safely poke a hole.

6

Twist the pencil between your hands to make the whole thing spin. Look through the slits to see your images move!

Shadow light show

Shine symbols and doodles onto a wall or ceiling with these cool cardboard projectors. They're really quick to make but provide hours of fun!

1 Place cellophane over the end of a cardboard roll and secure it with an elastic band.

Use a felt-tip or whiteboard pen to draw symbols or doodles onto the clear plastic. **2**

If you use a whiteboard marker, you can rub out your drawing and do a new one!

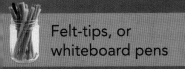

Felt-tips, or whiteboard pens

Torch (or you can use the torch on a phone)

Light projections

Light projectors can be used to project films onto screens at the cinema, light up buildings, and create art installations. **The Night Spectacular** is a light and sound show where lasers project images onto ancient buildings of Jerusalem to tell the tales of the city.

Turn off the lights. Place a torch inside the open end of the cardboard roll and switch it on, then point it at a wall or ceiling. You'll be able to see your drawings projected!

3

Templates

Clever camouflage, pages 102–103

Stick the two cut-outs together to create a cylinder.

Zoetrope, pages 128–129

Cut this template out twice. Then apply glue here and stick the two sections together.

Apply glue to the net
flaps to hold your
cube together.

Doodle cubes

pages 72–73

Lots of dots, pages 48–49

Did you know?

Learning about art encourages people to think more broadly about the world around them. Here are some fun facts about art and the people who make it.

Visiting a gallery

Many of the artworks in this book are on display in galleries around the world. Look up what galleries are near you and plan a visit! You could even take a sketchbook along to draw things that inspire you while you're there.

The White Cube Gallery, London, UK

Art jobs

As we've discovered in this book, art isn't only about being good at drawing. There are many jobs that require artistic skill. Here are just a few.

Graphic designers are responsible for the look and layout of things such as websites, books, posters, or magazines.

Craft makers design and create craft activities for magazines, websites, and books such as this one.

Art psychotherapists work in places such as schools or hospitals to help people use art to express their feelings.

Product developers plan and help design everything from clothes and hats to chairs and cars.

Art curators work in art galleries or museums and choose what type of artwork should be displayed and why.

Architects use their maths and drawing skills to design buildings and then oversee them being built.

Set designers choose the look and feel of a set on stage or on screen. They pick the props and how they are laid out.

Movements in art

There have been many different art movements, or types of art, throughout history. Which example from this book is your favourite?

Realism
The French artist Gustave Courbet led the Realism movement. He only painted what he could see in front of him.

Renaissance During this period, artists like Michelangelo painted portraits in more realistic ways than had been done before.

Pop Art
This began in the 1950s. Bold, bright colours were used by artists such as Andy Warhol to paint or print everyday objects.

The Bauhaus This art college in Germany was famous as a place to study, produce cutting-edge art, and have lots of fancy dress parties!

Child artists

The painter Pablo Picasso was what is known as a "child prodigy", as he was extremely talented from a very young age. He is said to have believed that every child is an artist. They are!

Making art is about trying new materials, experimenting, and having fun!

No clothes?

Many artworks show people without clothes on. Nude artworks help artists understand how to draw humans accurately.

The art of doing nothing

The performance artist Marina Abramović once did a piece of artwork where she sat in silence for 736 hours.

Glossary

abstract art Art style that uses shapes and colours rather than showing recognizable scenes or objects

activist Person who campaigns to bring about change

animation Sequence of images used to create a moving picture

array Arrangement of objects into columns and rows

batik Decorative method of dyeing cloth using wax

camouflage Colouring or markings that match an animal's surroundings, helping it to blend in

canvas Material stretched over wood to paint on

character Person featured in a story

collage Picture or design that uses different materials stuck on a surface

colour wheel Arrangement of colours in a circle, showing which colours complement each other

composition Placement of images in an artwork to give it a particular effect

Cubism Art style that uses geometric shapes

depth Artwork containing the appearance of distance

digital art Modern way of creating art, often using computer software

doodling Action of drawing without thinking about the end result

drawing machine Device used by artists to help focus on sections of a subject

ecological art Art about issues affecting the environment

elements of art Different effects, such as line, shape, pattern, tone, form, texture, and colour, that can be used in an artwork

exhibition Public showing of a piece or collection of artworks

fashion Popular styles of clothing

film frame Still image used to create a moving picture

flipbook Booklet with slightly different drawings on each page that when flicked through appear to move

form Object that is 3D

gallery Space where art is on display for people to view

geometric art Art style that uses straight lines, simple shapes, and bold blocks of colour

graffiti Marks, words, or images sprayed, stencilled, or painted on a surface in a public space

illustration Drawings that accompany text

installation Art piece that is often large-scale and 3D, arranged to fill a specific space

land art Art style where artists use natural materials

landscape Painting of scenery, such as mountains, rivers, trees, or fields

line Mark that is longer than a dot

marbling Effect that is created by swirling inks on top of water

marionette Puppet that is controlled from above using strings

mindfulness Paying attention to the present moment without distraction

modern art Art style that is less traditional than what went before; emerged in the late 19th century

Ndebele people Tribe of people who live in South Africa

net Flat shape that can be folded to make a particular 3D shape

Nōtan Artwork style that features light and dark designs, originating from Japan

Op Art Movement where artists created optical illusions in the 1960s

optical illusion Use of colour, light, and shape to trick the eyes

paper craft Making things from paper

pattern Colour or shape that is repeated

perspective Technique used to make an artwork look like it has depth

photojournalist Person who takes photographs to tell a story. Images might appear in a newspaper

Pointillism Painting technique that uses many small dots that merge to form a whole picture

portrait Painting of a person. Self-portraits are paintings by the artists of themselves

primary colours Three colours – red, yellow, and blue – that can be mixed together to form other colours

proportion Sizes of different parts of a whole in relation to each other

rangoli Traditional Indian pattern usually made with rice or sand

Realism Art style beginning in the 1850s, showing life in a realistic way

recycle Turn waste material into something new

reflective symmetry One side of a shape or artwork that is the same as the other

Renaissance Art movement between the 14th and 16th centuries, during which artists aimed to make their drawings more realistic using perspective

Romanticism 19th-century movement when artists painted in a bold, dramatic, or emotional style

rotational symmetry When a shape can be rotated and still look the same

sculpture 3D work of art

secondary colours Colours that are made by mixing primary colours

space Area inside or around a shape

stop motion Type of animation that shows an object or character move very slightly in each frame shot on camera

subject Something that the artist has chosen to draw, paint, or photograph

tessellation Shapes repeated to make a pattern without any gaps

texture How something feels to the touch

theme Idea or meaning behind an artwork

three-dimensional (3D) Solid shape or object that has height, width, and depth

tie-dye A method of dyeing material to make patterns

tone How light or dark an image is; can be used to make a shape look 3D

two-dimensional (2D) Shape or object that appears flat

vanishing point Imaginary point in a painting or drawing where the lines seem to come together as they disappear from view

weaving Creating material by interlacing fabric over and under itself

woodcut Block of wood used to print with

zoetrope Circular device which spins around and makes still images on the inside appear to move

Index

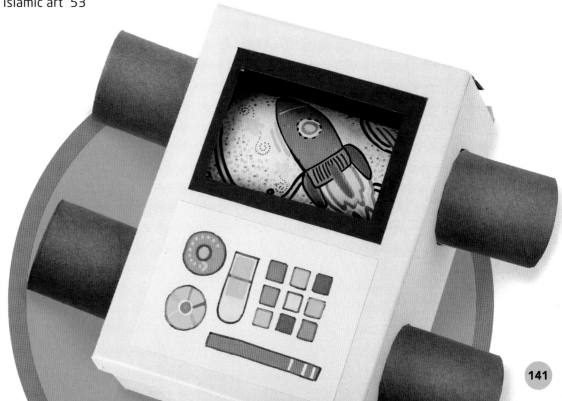

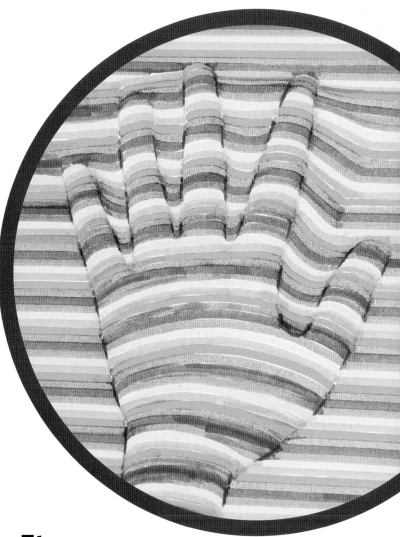

Acknowledgements

DK would like to thank the following: Caroline Hunt for proofreading; Helen Peters for the index; Lol Johnson for photography; Jaileen Kaur and Katherine Marriott for design assistance; Marie Greenwood and Katie Lawrence for editorial assistance; Evie Densham and Isla and Halle Trezel for modelling; Sophie Winder for craft assistance; and Anne Damerell for legal assistance.

S. Natalie Abadzis would like to thank: her parents Jo and Pierre, for always encouraging her to follow her dreams.